Near Camp ~~Gai~~ .... ~~s~~alut, whether cheese or navvy zone, Wayne Koestenba~~um~~ *~~C~~amp Marmalade* sits, lemony, curiously positioned, between epic alps and salty, notebook sound, i.e., tidbit *commedia*. Open to all comers, the camp is helmed by counselors (Duncan Smith, Friederike Mayröcker, and Lionel Hampton among them) who lead adventurers in a smorgasbord of activities, from "incest stardom fantasy" to "semantic depilation," from "dung oeuvre[s]" to directing "sunlight on slut emporia." After lewd s'mores, instead of "Taps" the assembled sing *"La Juive* 'Boléro'"* and call it a night—it's that kind of place. The "sieve of *I am*" has never produced a tenderer flower. —**Bruce Hainley**

To read *Camp Marmalade*, Wayne Koestenbaum's second "trance" epic, is to inhabit a mindscape, wordscape, and timespace increasingly rare and vital, in its emancipated sprawl, its dedication to "pleasing the gods of *weird* language" (think "shame bouillon" or "Yahweh's glitter"). Like Alice Notley's *Disobedience* or Hervé Guibert's *Mausoleum of Lovers, Camp Marmalade* is a fun house of fractal interiorities, via its assemblage of dreams, memories, observations, and idiosyncratic roll-calls (Vivien Leigh, Gwyneth Paltrow, Joyce Carol Oates, John Cage, Robin Williams, and countless others are here, not to mention Alessandro Scarlatti teabagging Jenny Craig). *Camp Marmalade*'s unfussy, deliberate rhythms and unstinting linguistic care feel like radical acts, offering pleasures of the highest order. —**Maggie Nelson**

Also by Wayne Koestenbaum

Double Talk: The Erotics of Male Literary Collaboration

Ode to Anna Moffo and Other Poems

The Queen's Throat: Opera, Homosexuality, and the Mystery of Desire

Rhapsodies of a Repeat Offender

Jackie Under My Skin: Interpreting an Icon

The Milk of Inquiry

Cleavage: Essays on Sex, Stars, and Aesthetics

Andy Warhol

Model Homes

Moira Orfei in Aigues-Mortes

Best-Selling Jewish Porn Films

Hotel Theory

Humiliation

Blue Stranger with Mosaic Background

The Anatomy of Harpo Marx

My 1980s & Other Essays

The Pink Trance Notebooks

Notes on Glaze: 18 Photographic Investigations

Camp Marmalade

Camp

Nightboat Books
New York

Wayne Koestenbaum

Mar-
malade

Copyright © 2018 by Wayne Koestenbaum
Printed in the United States

ISBN 978-1-937658-77-9

Designed and composed by Quemadura
Text set in Akzidenz and Didot

Cataloging-in-publication date is available
from the Library of Congress

Distributed by
University Press of New England
One Court Street
Lebanon, NH 03766
www.upne.com

Nightboat Books
New York
www.nightboat.org

for Steven Marchetti

Contents

Camp Marmalade

#1

[I despise always trying to be an intellectual]

        guy said "fag"
under his breath as I walked by

————————

        Sontag noted
"jam" means straight
in queer bar argot
(a "jam" life)—
she feared bathing—
I read aloud the last
paragraph of *The Volcano Lover*
("Damn them all")

————————

        Sonny Bono
met Shirley Jones and called
her "charming"

————————

and the revival of Gandhi's
homosexuality in old age—

———

screaming "help" in palsied
condition

———

I put
"penis" back into the
line after taking "penis"
(like a talking cure) out—

———

"don't patronize me," he
said, stapling my allure

———

for saying "don't
patronize me" I avoided him
forever—

———

"hungry i," where
Barbra premiered, three
years before labor pains

———

nylon-wearing
Cheryl, fourth-grade crush,
the girl I lost—why
did Cheryl's defection
puncture me and
serve notice of turn
away from popularity?

———————

stretch recalcitrant fabrics
and gesso them
in foretold patterns

———————

stain unprimed canvas with
poured acrylic, then gesso
the remaining unkind islands

———————

perforate a
drawing with electric stylus
and push pigment
through the tiny holes

———————

while I wait, I regret—
regret becomes the house and
not the subsidiary maisonette

————————

halfway ashamed of
the nightmare I dwell
within

————————

I was a young
mathematician (alias
Thaïs) at a school
with a high percentage
of suicides

————————

    ragged boys
standing on broken folding
chairs regard the philosopher
aiming a blow dryer

————————

    shame demands
immersion as swans

demand ponds, or as
urination demands
equilibrium—

———————

speaking German in the
Italian delicatessen

———————

is a mustache your
idea of heaven?

———————

lyrics reveal an
affair with Joni Mitchell

———————

         don't
make vague aesthetic
proclamations—
emphasize mental
illness quandaries, not
creative discoveries

———————

surviving the last
years before her death—

_____

deep dreams
about riding in a fancy
car with Sontag—

_____

his mustache
is missing, his mustache is
always missing or has been
missing for two sessions

_____

strong wish to donate
seed to the brilliant one,
though if the baby were mine
would I still find
him adorable? would I
find him incorrigible?

_____

when mood fails, when I
flee failed moods—

———————

when
pauses turn into
flower gardens—

———————

and the phrase
wooden teeth excised again and
again because it discriminates
against a woman or man
with wooden teeth—

———————

I despise
always pretending to be an
intellectual rather than
an assembler

———————

and the skinny German
in the porn shoot turned out
to be a fossil

———————

develop new ways to
become fluent in forgetfulness—

————————

his ekphrastic fixation
caused invisibility
to descend like a monsoon
over his tricks and milk,
his disappointing hygiene
and drums—

————————

      humming while she
gouges his gums—

————————

      babies aren't
racist, even if they stare

————————

we become a woman
taught in surgery
not to be a woman

————————

lumpy slow
men in medicated
cerebration

————————

Theda
Bara climbing toward lemon
groves—

————————

prosthetic interest versus
genuine interest, plunge
into actual material
versus spumante of wrong
inauthentic sparkling material—

————————

necking in
semi-public, I again
praised my phallus or
what passes as my
phallus and he said "anus"
as if I didn't have a headache

————————

disastrous plunge into
abyss, but what
is abyss and why do I
call it mother?

————————

         though his
mother belonged to Hitler Youth
he believes he was Jewish
in a past life

#2

[elegant toplessness stoned in stairwell]

they hated my poem about
a dead baby

_____

dead babies
in sonnets aren't funny

_____

I never said dead
babies were funny

_____

old man in wheelchair
falling over

_____

will the audience
misperceive my remark
as anti-Semitic
and boo?

———————

assemble an
entire life from found
scraps

———————

could my life
begin with the fat
girl babysitting while my
parents see *Odd Couple*
for their anniversary?

———————

kept boy follows
two steps behind doddering
master whose Cockney
S/M imprecations
toward rental dog
we overheard

———————

elegant toplessness
stoned in stairwell

———————

says hello at
deli, surprisingly high
voice for a grown son

—————

study
Diane Arbus for sake
of flirtation bait

—————

his ass
received verbal Nair,
semantic depilation

—————

"fold" I
said to Madame Grès

—————

dead man's
South Asian porn found
in grocery bags at gym

—————

did
lipstick on blind glamour
face repeal
the invisible city's
remaining condoms?

———————

Jim is
the repeated desired name
but a hollow resides
where Jim once lived

———————

LSD son
was Jim, a suicide, or rumored
to be a suicide in San Francisco

———————

erotic fantasy
of suicide nude hippie
answering Victorian
pink lady door

———————

his eyebrows deserve
dissection, troubadour
elegy

_____

four serried trees sublimely
waiting for me to announce them

_____

not convulsive beauty
but not obvious
beauty either

_____

     getting
stoned is the origin of
literature

_____

     or getting stoned by
angry homophobic journalists
and townspeople

_____

a pause
before I say yes despite
Elton John or
the mistreated girlfriend
who took it up the ass
from the sadistic boy
to avoid insemination

———————

this story told to me
as the height of her
humiliation or as symbolic
demonstration of my
cruel gay body's draconian
Rudolf Serkin willpower

———————

breasts felt
up by rival boyfriend
proved I was a noncontender

———————

upside-down mouth despite
zucchini-bread giftgiving

and *The Fox* reparations
on Third Street—my surprise
that San Jose had a good used
bookstore (I was an
impossible snob)

———————

why always is my suicide
fantasy poised on mother
of baby I adore more
than dignity allows?

———————

these questions are my
father's—precautionary,
nervous, dry, scape-
goated—

———————

     like the neighborhood
dog we feared

———————

I've never seen such a
compromised set of
lowhangers—

———————

    his pedagogic
illocutionary lowhangers—

———————

      or
Festschrift on my behalf
including Princess Di
eulogy

———————

    insane to
let him suck me off

———————

his persistence reminds me
of jilted Mary at mimeo
machine, stink of my cruelty

———————

not sure why
grease clings to my jacket
or why liberation is
achieved in unlikely locale

———————

brothers, together in tub
when father leaves,
experiment with rubber ducks

———————

snake joke on third-grade bus
counts as inaugural coitus lesson

———————

the stalled *Music Man*
bus where my first dis-
obedience broke its waters

———————

teaching Yahweh
about genitals,
grasping Yahweh's glitter

———————

lost thumb
of matzo ball purveyor
spooning goulash
near Hildegard Knef
LPs for sale
in thick plastic sleeves

#3

[nocturne for a cut-up dad]

      if his Wagnerian
dick were long and complicated
I could endure it

————————

imagine not surrendering
but forcing him to absorb
my aimed incursion
as slow penance

————————

      was her body
ever mine and soft and still,
la belle dame
kin as frigid likeness,
"commie" alabaster?

————————

      conifer tall
in Muir Woods—orthopedic-
shoes aunt we escort there

because she pays for Xmas coats
and every board game
in Kiddie World, including
Clue, Movie Moguls, Battleship

———————

I become sudden king
of board games through
Munich reparations
sent monthly to San Francisco

———————

supposedly according to
Siena and Mom I have
a "good mind" but I
know and many others know
I *don't* have a mind, or
else my mind isn't fit
company

———————

father capitulating
at New England beach or in forest—

_____

at rest-stop parking lot
mother confides in me
that father is capitulating—
I'm her co-conspirator
in task of regaining father

_____

    tired of trying
to assemble my face
through contortions into
faux handsomeness or
faux presentability—
it never works—

_____

    like Gatorade,
or *Wild Kingdom* at 7 pm
(a recipe for depression)
on Sunday, or Leslie
Caron as *Lili*, or *Kukla,
Fran and Ollie* anxiety

_____

on godless streetcorner
waiting for fake intercourse—
a Doug now dead
I once had delusional
(generic *Berkeley Barb*
radical body hair) lust for

—————

wanting him to return
for politico handshake,
to consider me a momentary
thin father, to stretch father
identity into a longer habitation—
nocturne for a cut-up dad

—————

nervous that
my method of describing
AIDS isn't the proper method
or that I'll use up
notebook before I get home or
that my heart will again become
a cage

—————

left side
of my face frozen from
fear of contact, stomach bulge
because shirt crumples

————————

sympathy with stroke's influence
on language—

————————

wolfed down a grilled
cheese and bacon
sandwich and weighed
131 last night

————————

don't denounce Maria
Lassnig for her self-
portrait in Vienna 1942—

————————

bitterness walking up 8th Avenue
in rain—teeth of
man selling newspapers—

he never cruises
me though I buy $1
water repeatedly

—————

heard Moffo *Faust* broadcast
also Mexico City *Traviata*
"Libiamo" 1961 with
Di Stefano—already
she must have been exhausted

—————

also heard *La Juive*
"Boléro," first recording ever
of *La Juive* "Boléro"—
it took more than
a century for *La Juive*
"Boléro" to be recorded—
leave it to 1974 to get some
important things accomplished,
like recording *La Juive*
"Boléro" (how many times
will I repeat *La Juive* "Boléro"?)

—————

severely damaging
my throat

———————

       was trance
the incentive, or stochastic
aim?

———————

       can intention
include the unaimed?

———————

       peregrinating
viola's unpredictable
Harold in Italy

———————

       stoic
conductor had temper
tantrums, our orchestra
didn't behave—

———————

oft-furious maestro
played *Thaïs* "Méditation"
violin solo in hippie
redwood mountain chalet

———————

irascible loyal maestro
imprisoned in Buchenwald,
fact revealed
only after his death

———————

obituary discovered
accidentally because
the word "stochastic"
instigated quest

#4

[essay on the shrug and the clutch purse]

Diogenes shitting in a
public place is the origin
of cynicism

————————

men of a certain vintage
naturally homophobic

————————

definition of homophone
is shaky

————————

 webbed fingers
of unseen captive girl
near dream bikeride

————————

beggar with luminous
crook face like Jack
Lemmon or Anthony Perkins

_____

I created Adam and
nothing came of it,
the Lord turned a page

_____

liquory voice of boy
who abused me,
sat on me—bedroom refuge,
refulgent balls on carpet

_____

sit with back against
wall to get Raphael Soyer
high bush—French horn player
witnessing trumpeter bush

_____

only
past bush is overpowering

_____

wife somehow
stinkier than husband

though both are stinky
by violin standards—
Eine kleine Nachtmusik
no one relishes

————————

told sexologist father
"I learned about VD
and phalloplasty
from your book"—

————————

she binds her breasts so
they won't be a nuisance

————————

      has mental
breakdown but calls it
merely emergency

————————

crust on leg, infected
pâte brisée

————————

vanished masseur, wastrel
with scarred face on Rentboy

———————

milkshake
at hilltop—we stand
to walk bike up steep incline

———————

both sides of
canvas belatedly revealed—
never to be a master

———————

speak honestly
about death on radio,
speak French to wrong bearded men

———————

death
of two elderly artists,
Sturtevant and Maria Lassnig—

———————

the word
I avoid is *starling*, to
say *starling* will ruin
the fragile ceremony—

_____

mourned boat
abandoned to its
rocking

_____

Lavinia
stump exeunt—

_____

then bedside
fellatio after Michaelmas fête
snub

_____

keeps pressing cock in
foyer, pseudo-succumb
because hard grope is easy
habit

———————

take testo
to counteract low mood

———————

le plan
cul is one-night stand

———————

inside Max Jacob is
a dropout stance, inside
Max find other phrases or
limbic openings

———————

say
the final "s"
in Duras—*due rass*

———————

pubic hair painted for first
time in ages—perhaps
return to fetishistic styles

———————

bias against
"as," a new rule, not
allowed (in the festival)
to use "as"

—————

wean myself from
anaphora and heavy breathing,
two wankers at Grand Central

—————

obituary updates, more
and more obits, Rossini's
grave accidentally and Colette's
and Wilde's

—————

mother threatens
to read my latest book
with magic machine

—————

I called three guys in a row
"stud" despite blinding sun

—————

lonely short-wave-radio
pals rendezvous at railway
atom-bomb outpost

_____

a Ferenczi essay on
the shrug and the clutch
purse

_____

      Westerns
stomached yet feared
as TV dinners are
feared for their foil trays

_____

why did he electrolysis
his juvenile arms?

_____

      dry hump
wise-incisors shrink
who speaks too softly
and exacts obeisance

#5

[the schmutz leitmotif]

don't fester in a
non-bold mode—
read Gramsci's
Prison Notebooks

———————

title for essay or poem—
Dude Awakening

———————

tired of my spine's
quest for
constant uprightness

———————

did she get her stomach
stapled, did I regress, how
is she only half her girth?

———————

large store-
bought canvases where all
events cohabit—

————————

sun returns, late
purple poppies wither—

————————

tautology, closed set—
terms create each
other and lead to dance,
a faith-based
system rather than a
narrative corridor
with exits and entrances

————————

a tone of vast fatigued
summational maturity, like
Stein in *Mother of Us All*—
"my long life"

————————

depressed
by careerism of others,
not depressed by careerism
of my own?

_____

bald spot in
elevator mirror a shock

_____

finished 130 pages
of anti-Semitic Céline

_____

I wasn't trayf, merely
pallor lying on pallet

_____

strive for a Jeff, intelligent
formalist face

_____

dream: molested a
baby by massaging him

twice—the first time
he liked it but then I
overstimulated him and
he shook and wept—

———————

he wasn't my kid, I
was babysitting him near
a photography conference—
I was keynote speaker

———————

eyelashes of Jewish
passerby

———————

Princess Di was my protégé's
kindergarten teacher

———————

    difference between
assumption and ascension—
when did Mary rise to heaven?

———————

I called my father "paranoid
old Jew" in reality,
dream, or short story

—————

given the chance we
explode into frenzied
underwear exploration,
schvitzing polyphony
in spike heels

—————

fake conviviality in the
coughing car

—————

       staccato
curiosity about Renata
Scotto's master
class with Warhol

—————

sneeze particles on
vulnerable love arm

———————

she has a hard time
giving or receiving love,
father said—did he mean sex
when he said love?

———————

mother threw wedding and
engagement rings in waste basket—

———————

"if I have success as a
poet, it won't be thanks to
any member of this family"—

———————

              a chance
to experience my mother's
soft skin when she was younger

———————

find a way of hugging
so stomachs and groins touch

———————

retreat to
mesmeric Tuolumne Meadows

———————

my 99th birthday and I'm
still quoting Wordsworth

———————

Nicolas Cage is a caption
for Susan Hayward

———————

                  the young
Fassbinder was (flashback)
handsome page-boy in
flapper Gertrude Lawrence
Star!

———————

       see *Star!*,
justify *Star!*, choose
Star!, lose *Star!*

———————

longing
to be a suicidal bikerider
on the Williamsburg Bridge

———

keep struggling with moonrise—
force yourself to have a
hard-on over moonrise,
see the moon fail to rise

———

Will Robinson
in *Lost in Space* is a
Scientologist and also
a good kid, a psycho gem—

———

is he the little boy I abused
in the dream? wrung him
dry by massaging
him for pleasure I knew
how to give easily

———

privacy
issues of massaged baby

———————

cinnamon means anus smell
eroticized and commodified

———————

no forgiveness for war
crimes—mother is my
war crime, our
behavior together is war
crime (exaggeration)

———————

dreamt two
little babies crawled on
top of me—was I
consoling them or were
they consoling me?

———————

ordered steak tartare
and then strip steak with

side of potatoes rösti, obscene
lack of vegetables—"I hate
fennel" he said

————————

                couldn't figure
out how to draw redhead
I thought would be easy

————————

        straight Jew
pianist stubble, hypnotic jam,
gaze too avid

————————

Autism the only book I wanted
in the dead woman's household

————————

        to pity or
fear the schmutz leitmotif

————————

the less attractive ones are
sexier, you can imagine them
going lower

—————

can't fit into white
pants or almost can't—
finally squeezed my hips in

—————

"contact high
from your manliness" I
said to child psychologist

—————

bought
watch I think is a woman's

—————

perfect teeth of guy
who sold me woman's watch

#6

[Smoky Legs]

"you have nice breasts" he said—
"but sir" (I corrected him)
"I don't have breasts"

———————

Schumann's commedia-dell'-
arte theme of cranky pupil

———————

Artur Schnabel
student moaning after
shameful *Waldstein* sonata

———————

Carole
King's Gerry Goffin died
today—I always confused
him with David Geffen

———————

listened thrice to *Love of Three Kings*
for greatest amour's death

_____

"I'm going to record *Norma*
with the London Symphony"
she said on radio interview—
delusion?

_____

      Horace Silver died—
revere his 1950s sides

_____

not every beard is gay though
we misjudge possessors

_____

remembering her mother
cruel in Far Rockaway—
its geographical
relation to Greenwich Village
incomprehensible

_____

my job is to learn Hebrew
and your job is to understand
why I am learning Hebrew

———————

speak of
Eichmann please in the
past tense unless this is
a one-act play

———————

we become an "it" moralist,
we moralize pronouns,
we atomize pronouns, uttering
a droplet version of "he" and "she"

———————

taking her arm
to cross street—am I protecting
grandmother or is she
protecting me?

———————

touching grandmother's hair
and saying "cotton candy"—
did I ask before I touched?

———————

remembering the couch
where I touched
grandmother hair

———————

remembering whitefish
exotic in deli envelope

———————

a face so leaden I gaze
at the ocean instead

———————

      wondering
if father owns the basement
or if father sometimes lives
in the basement

———————

remembering
kitchen's orange bar stools—
loving orange but knowing
orange is vulgar or wrong or us

_____

we are orange people—orange
defines our otherness and rage

_____

mother is
more orange than father—
father (as I have told
you) is green—brother
is beige—sister is yellow—

_____

a woman or
girl screaming because she
doesn't understand her
physical distress—responding
to flow she starts screaming

_____

one of those uncanny children
in Hitchcock

———————

      hearing mother
throw *The Reproduction Story*
into my room—I'm in the
bathtub and I hear her proclaim
the book now my property—
tactic to punish brother—

———————

remembering moles on her
upper arms, underarm shave
dots, area where
arm meets sleeveless blouse

———————

     rings in
bureau dish—top drawer
pulls out to reveal
inset tray containing coins
and clip-on earrings

———————

opening closet, seeing dresses—
don't remember father's clothes

—————

smell of baby brother's
teddy bear and blanket—
no smell of older brother—
only person who has a
smell is baby brother and
his smell (porridge) is good

—————

remembering look of phone
off the hook, busy signal
beep a terror warning

—————

remembering
father Phi Beta Kappa
photo, his face not making sense

—————

remembering
redwood fence

rust—other families had
Mercurochrome, I wanted
it but suspected
the remedy was flawed—

_____

emotion lavished
on *Volete la mia vita*
when Moffo sings the explosive
phrase—give her more
credit for ending career
with unquenched verismo

_____

      Henry
James felt faint in George Eliot's
presence—they worshipped together—

_____

two salesmen treated
me without love—I start to
doubt the store's morality

_____

Henri
Lefebvre dropped from my lap
when I fell asleep—
intrusive stranger woke me
to point out Lefebvre fallen
onto schmutzy floor—

————————

delirium of not knowing
how to frame or contextualize
the process

————————

he became my seventh-grade
English teacher by suddenly
squinting—they had in
common a red beard

————————

not wanting to insert my
dick after bravura
cunnilingus—being
told I have a low sex drive—

————————

my repeated strident
proclamations (effusions?)
about adjacency, contiguity

———————

condensing self-pity into
medicated lozenges—loving
the Sucrets box too much—
choosing ignominy
as a new green

———————

is D. W. Winnicott more
famous than D. W. Griffith?
Broken Blossoms
versus holding environment—
Orphans of the Storm
versus good enough mother—

———————

she told me I had
a good enough mother and then
rescinded the sanguine diagnosis—

———————

imagine
Joyce Carol Oates fantasizing in a white-
carpeted office, hour after hour

———————

Paganini and
Artaud had no teeth

———————

I chew on my students

———————

remembering
sudden light outside
shut bedroom door and
remembering bedtime's revocation

———————

remembering my problem
closet, out of date and ruined—

———————

book I thought
free turned out to be
constricted Ashkenazi tsunami

————

93-year-old Julius
Rudel died

————

cookout near Lawrence Expressway,
frenchkissing at burger
vault with twin—
the less pretty one—

————

their divorce
house one street
south of bowling alley

————

fingers in bowling ball,
dark restrooms at
Brave Bull near Pall Mall
and Lucky Strike machine

————

Fourth of July
depression, worms
in front yard, sparklers in back

———————

a downstairs dwarf
telephoned to complain
that my thumping
woke her up—

———————

      early evening
mother naps on couch—lying
down to watch Julia Child—

———————

confused by Jack LaLanne's
couture and plotlessness

———————

tanned block lady Judy
in hot pants—we named her
"Smoky Legs" because she smoked—
we thought cigarettes
bronzed her legs—

———————

mountain, we don't
worship you—rock piles
without meaning

_____

imaginary
baby clutched on idiot lap

_____

Rita Hayworth's real
name is Realm

_____

my second-grade
teacher Miss Paul
got married and became someone
else—I'll never know who
Miss Paul became

#7

[insta-hard pickle bowl slowpoke catharsis]

rituals give pleasure but
also we receive pleasure
from destroying ritual

_____

use large arm movements
or be content with small

_____

curator said "this
is the tittie room" and I
repeated "tittie" which is
OK once or twice but I
repeated "tittie" four times

_____

I'm insta-hard—does he
feel the insta-hard?—

_____

regret not extending the hug
another five beats

_____

                shows
me blue ankles and blue
legs and I'm stuck with them

_____

         ecocide toward
my infant self, incinerate
infancy, damage the coverlet
I slept in—cascade
into infanticide fantasies
congealed into a Gothic novel

_____

tendency to press doesn't
lead to good results and yet
I keep pressing—obliteration
of mental keenness is a skill

_____

mother papers the filthy
bottoms of daughter's
dorm-room bureau drawers—

———————

father says "your
mother burst into tears
when your plane took off"

———————

did she mistake me
for stillborn boy or girl?
my resemblance to a
dead baby is keen

———————

      my gift for
betrayal approaches
Azucena's, who
sets fire to her own child

———————

for Jewish retrospection
I order pickle bowl

————————

                 urine
droplet in red undies
because I tuck in
too quickly—ineligible
for hottie sweepstakes

————————

Gertrude Stein had an
American accent when
she said goodbye in French

————————

        scar
marks on crematorium
interior appear as greeting
page

————————

Allen Grossman died today

————————

night and day go orange
on me—inspired by hearses

———————

took off his shirt on 23rd
Street to show new
tattoo—I touched it—
"I know what you're packing"

———————

developing
blindisms involuntarily

———————

dreamt of a barely
housebroken dog, a half-
loved Martian

———————

Bunny
Megabunny was my brother's
most charismatic stuffed animal—

———————

Paul Mazursky died, broken Bob
and broken Alice—

———————

painted toenails of little girl
in high heels—time to watch
Pretty Baby and be jealous
of Brooke Shields

————————

for five minutes I can
lift mother's mood—

————————

depression when a baby
cries, a whelp-naught,
a *noeud* of quails

————————

we live for the three minutes
leading to orgasm's opium

————————

a fake
Ravel sonata is better
than no Ravel

————————

stretching
canvases, slowpoke
catharsis

———————

sparkling penis in piñata,
autophagous circumlocutions

———————

Vic Mature's
nature-lovin' porch phase, smoking
grass in Flatbush and reading
Canterbury Tales aloud for
three hours as shrine—

———————

Nadal trounced
by nineteen-year-old,
but Nadal is cuter than
the new young star

———————

a likeness to Loch Ness,
Lakmé's lox

————

　　　full
as an *Ungeziefer*, or
whatever Kafka calls his
Gregor-bug—always saying
Ungeziefer or Anselm Kiefer at
dinner parties as solution
to repartee quandaries

————

　　　Jason Gould again
as incest stardom fantasy

————

stuttering professor who
taught me how to read
poetry slowly
quickly dead (brain
tumor) at 33—
very dead now, more dead
now in 2014 than when
he died in 1980

#8

[Burger Pit a scene of forgiveness]

I said three cheers for
calf worship when the calves
are yours and I'm the worshipper—

—————

she
in fuchsia onesie sits beside
me—we're tied
by shared aversions

—————

limp wrists
autistic—playing strange games
with shapes in sidewalk,
touching every bubble

—————

saw
Love Story with mother
and she called me Preppie

henceforth as affectionate
nickname—also called me
Buster Keaton

_____

              did he
show me the nude drawing
a student gave him? unlisted
phone number to avoid midnight
calls from jilted nympho protégées

_____

never smile willingly, never gush,
be formal—eyes warm yet dead

_____

         there once was an
ugly lamb, no one loved
the ugly lamb, the ugly
lamb went to Sunday
School and opened his
World's Fair lunchbox

_____

I felt sentimental about
my chicken and avocado
sandwich because the
bread was not lousy—
the space between
rotten and decent was
Weltschmerz domain—

———————

open your mouth wide,
say "ah" and let cheap
thrills enter

———————

begin undressing in aisle on
way to bathroom,
diseased leg purple

———————

I objectify by saying "you're
adorable," breasts thunked
together—can you *thunk*
or think a breast,
not gendered?

———

mother fed me raw egg yolk
milkshake when ill

———

block lady dying was
yellow—her two daughters tended
toward green—

———

proselytizing friend grows
psychotic or paranoid while
driving car from Santa Cruz

———

no longer consider speech
incarcerating but don't
idealize speech

———

charismatic
a tadpole word thrown
into the orgy—sexual mistakes
with lounging out-of-towners

———————

aerosol whipped cream
sprayed into my mouth

———————

pianist bride breasts high
beneath implied mustache
and I am twin of groom
who wore falsies and had
a TV variety hour
devoted to falsies, radioactive
Samson and Delilah

———————

lounging in Mediterranean
briefs, large and lazy balls
express no curiosity
about their own largeness

———————

touch daughter's breasts solely
for séance with her famous mother

———————

massage parlor became
dead haircutter's echo salon—
did echo salon always
carry imminent death taint?

———————

caught with sick man
vomit pail during socializing,
serving him chickpea and pasta
soup with intermission
for vomit pail—

———————

was Burger Pit
a scene of forgiveness?
block ladies and Thousand Island
at salad bar where first
lessons in nutrition
and clemency took place—

———————

mother's finger in heated
milk saucepan to test
temperature, abstract finger

————————

Mae West poster
ripped up—witnessing
destruction—terror at seeing
my bodyguard lose control

————————

why didn't they
advise me to cut my hair?

————————

Bing cherry orchards
spied from Rambler station wagon
a first lesson in parallelism

————————

weeping boy
on father-therapist's Sonny
Bono lap

————————

on and
off goes the silent Walpurgis-
nacht Kindertotenlieder porno
playing pattycake

#9

[maybe she exaggerates her bladder emergency]

constant crying of not cute
enough baby, unformed mouth

_____

French children behave,
play in dirt and consider it
grass or sand, play in mud
and consider it ocean

_____

      when he pressed
leg against me—
was I the provoker,
and he the theorist of my
provocation?

_____

      grammar school
vomit as covert communication

_____

crass
group laughter implying
consensus—does consensus lead
to bullying, or is bullying
a solo operation?

———————

cold baby today I want
to give you an
early Kir to prepare
for a later lifetime
of Kirs—

———————

afraid of unloved
leaping kitten—
if kitten enters kitchen
I'll be accountable
for its unlove invasion—

———————

did Tante commit suicide?
never told the cause
of death—no funeral—

reparation checks
opulent or meager

———————

she covered
my eyes against 1960s
San Francisco porn marquees,
sunlight on slut emporia

———————

death
wind on scalp, repeated
Rambler sirocco—

———————

Childwold summer confusion,
fantasy that Oates will be
my 1977 conduit
upstairs to mother

———————

depress the silver obedience
woodwind valve

———————

concentrate on jowl
prevention tips

————————

I see his elaborate
punishment bracelet and wish
to be his temporary underling—

————————

big woman
running to back
of airplane, she's not
allowed to, what if she
pees in the aisle

————————

maybe she exaggerates her
bladder emergency—

————————

small white earrings
of imminent bladder shame
and I must witness it and
empathize, experience

it as fellow torment—

_____

announce a bladder need
and then be stigmatized
as the one who announced it—

_____

TB TB
burning bright—

_____

      eager to see
a young male (35 is
young) stomach when he
raises arms to fix *parapluie*

_____

          dreamt
Callas was a back-up
singer in *a cappella* Moffo
Traviata, late '6os

_____

face of Dr. Watson who
brought me into the world

———————

imitating father by writing
in diners—Denny's, Big Boy

———————

encounters with
white toast on the side,
sliced encounters, over easy

———————

becoming a
writer through repetition and
persistence and not thinking,
becoming a person of few words,
cinder-burdened

———————

flutter of imminent flirtation
and the *Music Box* movie
daughter discovering father's
Nazi past

———————

I owe him—debt
is a chuppah
I stand under to marry
my own self-disgust

———————

      erotic cosmopolis
dream shattered and its
shattering becomes yet another
chuppah I stand beneath

———————

mother's beige wedding dress,
block lady Rose attends ceremony
and then dies

———————

self-belief is father's
nuclear accelerator

———————

the good side of your dead father
was his narrative flair

––––––––––

why do
ladykillers desire my proximity?
are they tired of ladykilling
and want to begin Jewish
gay male poet killing?
am I a reverse Lulu?

––––––––––

found sadomasochism one
1970s Chicago summer
and then threshed
Christ in the *Nachlass* dungeon—

––––––––––

they smile at me as if I
were their private movie star,
cold beard mouth
set like obsidian
without animation

––––––––––

discover genealogy of
Tante's phrase *come good home*,

like *make good again,*
Wiedergutmachung, again
good make, as if original home
(pre-Nazi) were good
and we could return there

———————

large charcoal eyes
immediately win boyfriends

———————

       son
has saint tattoo on
Reichs-Theater calf—

———————

do I stay here forever with
bacon in father's wine garden?
or better to emulate Vanessa
Redgrave dizzy
walking downtown, scrutinizing
lexical imagination's shadows

———————

stepfather cuddled you
I remember you confessed
lightheartedly

———————

     Fassbinder's
wives considered him sexually
attractive, towel around neck

———————

        dreamt
top-notch art gallery sold
clothing at cut-rate
prices, $6 Viennese
sweaters—climb a ladder to
reach cheap luxury

———————

     leaf bole rot, *etwas*
leaf balm rote walk,
langsam Brando mint
chamomile, *mille grazie*
etwas Brando leaf mote
rot

———————

      I sent him
"Depuis le jour"—lyrics
cribbed from incest's
book, frontispiece
dying baby mannequin

———————

nimble husband with sports
bra adds up to urination
Dayenu coloratura,
his bubble tea pre-cum orange

———————

HIV reappears in cured baby

———————

kill flies, see babies come out—
misty Coronet documentary diorama

———————

google his horny homophobic
stepfather to compile
catalogue raisonné
of cute stepson's sorrow

#10

[swaddled by screw-worthiness]

facing a Cool Whip
medical condition

⸺

       bearded
seer whose stomach my
stomach pressed

⸺

    Liz's face raised
to catch sunlight, violet eyes
closed

⸺

upper lip fetish zone of 1988
intact though glare-blinded

⸺

scolded by summer
stock director Jim

for cracking up onstage—
Jim reappeared to defend
Gay Deceivers skit banned
by junior-high VP

————————

dad-underbrush is
wobbly and undescribed

————————

clipped Genet's
obituary, Baldwin's

————————

stubble knew itself
superior and could be resented

————————

terrified of showering in
public, hired prostitute

————————

gave two dollars to
woman with AIDS to buy Subway
sandwich—she said she liked my hair

———————

in 1985 found the word "greaves"
through discipline and then chance

———————

Oh, qual pallor
three-year-old girl's David
Bowie impersonation

———————

handsome man's absorption in his
own private activity is a dad wall

———————

didn't understand high
school cult of thesis
statement written in
advance of essay itself
on *Cry, the Beloved Country*

———————

I heard Renée Fleming
say "multi-task" in her
Connecticut house

———————

      Christoph Eschenbach's
performance of Mozart's F
major concerto #19—ontological
debris of dad knowledge

———————

little boy hugs me because I
slept with sperm donor—
kid smells familiar spunk on me,
a road shaped like a crucifix

———————

brother wants his servitude to stop—
I culpably sculpted it

———————

you influenced me a lot says dad
with curly hair—memorize the
playful influence and scatter it

———————

to dwell within impatience's
germinating soil,

to explain the groove carefully
without telling the reader what
a groove is or why
we should care about grooves

—————————

     not to be screwed by
him but to be encircled
by his wish to screw
and by every sign that
in and on his body connotes
worthiness to screw—
to be swaddled
by screw-worthiness

—————————

     his brother tried
to play piano but had a disability
the mother discussed in public

—————————

right now his balls (whose?
everyone's) are vivid to me
she wrote or I did also

———————

he'll take a night off
from screwing and offer gratis
balls to assuage
my bunkbed melancholy—

———————

automatic trash congress
on towels

———————

    gender-
hacked dad, jaundiced, royal—
quiet kid watching
snippets of found blow

———————

    change
purse bends with difficulty to
open its plastic mouth, agony
of dad's change purse

———————

to avoid logic for an entire
lifetime is a crime

---

disappointed that I started a
big painting by sketching a large
demented face, Mia Farrow's new
barechested baby look

---

      recovering
from Gianni Versace's murder,
recovering from anyone's murder

---

garage door falling on my head
a school day event

---

is Paul Goodman forgotten?
bonus pile of Goodman juvenilia

---

artist shows me sex photo—
I compliment his thigh,
his broken Roman
nose, his girlfriend's breasts

and slim waist—I say "it looks
like you're going to cum in
15 seconds"—his eyes in the
photo are closed

—————————

      is he a hustler?
he was disappointed when I
told him I wasn't rich—
he said "I'm an ass man,"
I didn't say what I was

—————————

*Decline and Fall of the Roman
Empire* as index of Onassis
eschatological consciousness

—————————

         I lose
interest in writing when skinny
ass steps away—want to see
him scratch his belly

—————————

grandmother was
saintly and orthodox and I
eat hamburger as response to
grandmother's crabbiness

_____

asking forgiveness
for not wanting the smelly

_____

mother is
the door I opened to
enter the world
but she is no longer the door

_____

translate light
blue chalk of red brick

_____

door-to-door selling Christmas
cards and *Reader's Digest*—
I sold only one subscription,
to Tante Alice

———————

looked on ground for coins as
moneymaking scheme,
garage 8mm nickelodeon—
idolized two-story houses

———————

why always ultramarine as island
of belated decisiveness amid funk
and diseases of the will?
acedia, abulia

———————

dong shown while he lolled on
toilet seat, almost homo action
when babysitter barged in

———————

        baby cry is
knife to repulsed consciousness—
crossed leg is Tyrone Power
unlaughter pogrom

———————

                    stoned
in Berkeley bathroom I
telephone potential trick
who describes his chest as hairy
only because I ask him if
he has a hairy chest so of
course he corroborates
my fantasy—

————————

good night Elaine Stritch good
night Judy Garland good night
one-point perspective Duccio
Giotto mannerists figuring out
light Georges de La Tour and fore-
shortening, good night Tintoretto
Veronese and the sublimating
summarizing impulse

#11

[slaughter ball]

I promised him
an ode, "Jared
stubble in parfumerie"

—————

enjoy the bumps
obstructing cognition—

—————

two or three
roses beautiful because
they are separate from
each other—separated
roses are more beautiful
than joined roses

—————

she'd never
heard of sugar snap
peas—I explained
sugar snap peas in detail

———————

imbibe straight male
narcissism, see how
it tastes and sounds

———————

Elaine
Stritch died yesterday,
89—see mother once more
before she turns 84

———————

hooked on Cheops

———————

my hand lit up and
crammed into you

———————

or Schoenberg's
waxed bikini line
redux, trilling like Romeo

———————

          nonstop
Otello storm clouds,
his fat unshaved
chops sucking storied
lollipop

———————

          nose of
96-year-old blind
mother of anyone,
a face moving
into early dementia

———————

dementia at
96 isn't early

———————

I like the word "stipple"
I say at lunch

———————

common for sons
to be sued for defamation

of character—I have
thrice been tried

—————

aunt whose last shame
before death is witnessing
the mayo bologna fight

—————

no pee coming from Fed Ex
man at urinal, I linger
by sink and allow silence
to blossom so his pee-
shyness can grow audible—

—————

maybe upper-middle-
class dad will smother
the baby—

—————

your near-
death experience
involved a wall
of grape hyacinths

———————

identification with crying
baby but also a wild
wish to stop the crying
by stopping the baby's
existence

———————

vielleicht the baby
is a future war
criminal

———————

her name is Aurore
Clément—she
plays the mother in
Chabrol's *Bridesmaid*—

———————

I added Venetian
red which is really
brown to create an
illusion of ground
beneath a car

———————

added ultramarine blue
above the car and
accidentally effaced
purple coneflower stems

————

        then dragged
a pencil through
pink to retrieve
lost lines of two
figures coitally embroiled

————

        and now I
see a rhubarb-colored
dodge ball (slaughter ball?)
balanced between two
mustard lines—

————

skillfulness abides in
seemingly random and
unthought decisions—

————

deliberation,
if it occurs, must
itself be spontaneous—

———————

I won't
ask him to pose—
asking involves
a level of abjection
even I am incapable
of descending to—

———————

though
deciding I won't ask
fills me with teen
despair—father's
fullness reigning
over me with titanic
indomitability—

———————

my recourse
to code situates

me as Satan, not
major-domo Satan but
Satan's little helper
with an apron and
thimble and food
processor for slicing
carrots on the bias—

———————

Josep
Pla's anti-Semitic description
of Jewish necks—

———————

caught having sex with a
guy at 17, pants opened,
dicks out, taunted for
a year

———————

an edible
crawling tortoise
we ran over and couldn't
eat the murdered meat

———

wanton destructiveness
toward my private
property—

———

    a problem
for five decades, these
objective unlyrical statements

———

maybe gradually caress
his arm to receive
touch backward

———

scarf by Vera a status
symbol in Coral Gables
or towns that yearn
to be Coral Gables

———

cross out a big area
with bilge and then
write on top of the bilge

———————

     headed
toward hell, saying
please to hell as I approach
its ambiguous gate—
or is hell a river?

———————

     in the Hill
Korwa tribe's drawings,
an alphabet wordlessly
emerges

———————

a non-gay-seeming
man was holding hands
with a gay-seeming man near
the ragtag pharmacy

#12

[the dematerializing marzipan]

spit on every painting so
I can list saliva as
ingredient, also use
cum in every painting
as underlayer

_____

fun hierarchies versus
dung hierarchies

_____

I defend little girl's
dung penis

_____

my dung oeuvre like
Racine's *Phèdre* intoning
dis-je dung, *dis-je*
Phèdre at a dung
ristorante

———————

      he deleted
his GayRomeo profile
and I lost him forever
on Portugal beach—he
became a novel of favors
rescinded

———————

      reviewer unkindly
panned Woody Allen movie—
why always pan Woody
just because you don't
approve of his sexual arrangements?
I know child molesting
isn't a sexual arrangement
but no one proved that Woody
was a child molester

———————

      ombudsman
to her Joplin piano
breasts in Karmann Ghia—
I mean Janis Joplin, not Scott

_____

Travis was our sexual glue,
he'd hire Travis and I'd
watch, or I'd hire Travis first

_____

extend filth into a novel
and then suck the novel's failure

_____

       again Baked Alaska
trace of nostalgia for
murdered classmate whose mother
wrote me to say her hitchhiking
daughter had been killed

_____

       father begged for
marzipan—did he pretend
to love marzipan so we kids
had something inexpensive
to buy him?

_____

mother
never bought him marzipan—
did he ever buy it for himself?

———————

why did
marzipan always come
in trompe l'oeil shapes—
Elvis Presley, carrot,
car, Colosseum, tulip?

———————

marzipan was a joke
food, sold at underdog shops—
no normal stores sold it

———————

my sentimental
love for him centered
on his supposed love
of marzipan and the
ease of satisfying him
by buying him marzipan
though it remained a

mystery whether he
actually loved marzipan

————————

maybe he secretly threw it away—
it disappeared shortly after
we gave it to him—
the dematerializing marzipan

————————

      skinny-dipping at gay
B&B, Berkshires,
schnapps ice-cubes in tap water—

————————

Russian pianist belly by
epileptic river—
shorthand like shame bouillon—

————————

jetting euphemism isolates
cum for extermination—
keep mentioning extermination
because it's real, what

he suffered under, and
his suffering (even if he
only rarely mentioned it)
became mine—

———————

dead boy
revenant, stop knocking
on my bedroom window—

———————

men who demote me
are the ones I desire—
rejection's aphrodisiac

#13

[I agree to be her cesspool]

butt contact with aggressive
crazy man who said "dude"
angrily to anonymous busker—

—————

Victor Hugo was
Warhol's finest erotic subject

—————

Cather's recorded tribulations
hardly domestic in their
entirety—nor Munro's—
don't condescend
to "domestic" subjects—

—————

I agree to
be her cesspool so she
won't spill it on others—

—————

someone called her hair
or mine a rat's nest—

———————

I typed madly for
stiff Finnish wife
in dark house Xmas—
Midlothian not finished,
intimacy on rug

———————

      watching
a guest-star cameo
performance of me
becoming a detested
person like vanishing
point at end of Natalia
Ginzburg's "Mother" story

———————

      at health-food store
my $1.50 check for tea bags
bounced

———————

when lawn Frisbee nude
was campus king—

_____

      never figured
out the difference between
I. Magnin and Joseph Magnin—
one store was the origin of
fancy puppets in gold box—

_____

puppet theater, her gaze
as I open Xmas present

_____

      time spent forming
sentences versus leaving
sentences unformed

_____

          Bus
Stop Marilyn's bid for
seriousness, rarely accorded

_____

brother is
teal—I saw long ago
his teal essence

———————

the two motel
rooms of anus and vagina
have very thin adjoining
walls

———————

and the
failure to see my sister
perform in high school
Once Upon a Mattress,
inexcusable omission though
I lived 3,000 miles away

———————

dreamt the director wet
my bed and didn't cast me
in her budget documentary—
I told her she was rude—
she threw me 30 euros

———————

                    no
that's not my mustache,
I've never had a mustache,
I left the brown there
and the brown simulated
a leftover mustache

———————

          no escalator
in Baudelaire though I
hallucinated a department store
"Harmonie du soir"

———————

          nun holding
cake box tied with blue
string

———————

suspicious cut on thumb
as madeleine gateway

———————

Carlo Bergonzi died—
obit exaggerates
final *Otello* fiasco

———————

the Amneris
of Everard Baths

———————

check the void,
see if the void's still
there, still breathing—

———————

the void's undulating
buttocks soothsay

———————

open up your buttocks
to invasive wetness
of failure to be cast in
Fassbinder-esque documentary
noir dream—

———————

one beard tinged with
falseness, the other beard true

———————

his square face
is gum to me,
I chew it as mental image

———————

      grandfather's death
happened on telephone

———————

like Maya Deren I said,
or Chantal Akerman's
use of Aurore Clément

———————

many astute people, men
and women, found a use
for Aurore Clément

———————

we do not yet fully
understand Aurore Clément

—————

captivated by my ignorance
of Aurore Clément's career
and significance, the going-
in-circles of Aurore Clément

—————

hi Timmy by osmosis
became the next sentence

—————

San Jose
library suddenly architecturally
distinguished, like Bibliothèque
Sainte-Geneviève

—————

the girls appreciate
Stein, the boys don't

—————

Schwinn bike
a Xmas gift stolen—
one morning too lazy
or depersonalized to lock it

———

sit outside on bench
while hair dye settles,
sun on naked scarred leg

———

sunbathing in backyard
while Sutherland *Linda
di Chamounix* plays through
sister's bedroom window

———

ashamed of my small
diseased eyes in mirror

———

insect sludge dripped
down my neck

———

shouting "I
can't stand scholars!"

———

124

or "crouched in a defensive
posture"—"crouch" seems
anti-Semitic—inwardness
homophobically slammed

———————

Heffalump, my brother's
Australian stuffed animal,
worked as an airline
pilot or else was
just a lively passenger—

———————

            when
my brother and I ran away
to an imaginary airport three
blocks distant, Rhonda Drive,
we brought Heffalump—
in Australia we'd speak
uselessly our nascent French

———————

        eau in
nausea imagines ocean

is latent (or immanent)
in self-loathing—
nautical vistas hallucinated
within self-disgust's
dressingroom full-length mirror—

#14

[tight ultramarine fealty to wimp identity]

sitting at counter, I ate
smoky avocado wrap
while watching lurching
man nearly faint,
trying to rest his
lanky strung-out body
on U.S. postal worker

———————

Huppert apparently
gave him a "withering look"
backstage at *The Maids*

———————

mystery guy
with tight ultramarine
jeans sneezes

———————

squeezes
cold grey around orange areas

———————

in a few he will smell of
the artist whose goth
tendencies and reticence
earn my affection—

———————

why always goldenrod or
golden hair as in
Celan's "Todesfuge"?

———————

     thorough
citation makes me slow
down—

———————

     JFK Jr. photos released
in black and white

———————

     everyone on
the Rambla trying to sell me
cocaine in 1919

———————

today "we" bomb
Iraq again—no
clean way to say it

———————

handwashing protocol of
Agnes Moorehead in *Magnificent
Obsession*, great moment
of sanitary fussiness, she'll
do sight-restoring
operation on Jane Wyman but
first must sterilize
soon-to-be-*Bewitched* hands

———————

Broadway, 1965—
Liz arriving at *Hamlet*,
sidewalk mob
like *Children of Paradise* finale—

———————

I said you are my godmother,
and the beauty trained
on me a glance

she's accustomed to giving
the non-famous, the non-
handsome, the non-impeccable—

—————

    I mimic
a buzzard's metronomic tact

—————

"this is she" said the girl who
refused me on the phone—
in class, her slip showed
beneath dress hem—

—————

    search
for sexual maturity in girls
governed me

—————

        something
Dalton Trumbo about this
procedure, sir—
whose resonance will go
unwept—

———————

dangerous when a crush is
reciprocated—some reciprocated
crushes turn into open
warfare

———————

notice the hole
through which the status pours

———————

butcher thinks I'm a good cook
because I ask for pork tenderloin

———————

taking a whizz on
batik never tucked
into morgue couch

———————

but my
fealty extends to wimp
identity

———————

we smell like a
rutting ox—if oxen rut—
a stranded abstraction

————————

appreciating
the messy Giacometti because
its design is unpredictable
and unparaphrasable

————————

brought to
pedagogical symposia on Saturday
mornings to prove that little
boy trumpeters could improvise—
"tell a story on your trumpet"—

————————

watching *Follies* for
the urge to omit plot

————————

the story of Joan Crawford's Pepsi
phase intersecting with *Big Knife*
Ida Lupino orgasmatron

    ————

      the son loves to
be confused with the husband,
very Erving Goffman, very
Partridge Family

    ————

in the style of Comme
des Garçons *Tristan*
I never recovered
from my gay husband dumping me
meteoric in café
astride the Koons agon

    ————

don't you dare begin to
grunt—a steady state of
grunting that passes
for intellection

    ————

         unforgivable to
ignore or organize Andrew Lang

red fairy fugues—he fugues
for a fairy living like
Wilde's wife

————

or Freud's
fantasy of impregnated Leonardo

————

witches, their
souls are rum, the commute
of random witch souls ah!

————

she suicides monthly to break
duration

————

Lupino
directs *Hitch-Hiker* and clones
Johnny Weissmuller, straight guy
Ironside child-bloom

————

repeated unconscious
asters etched

—————

like Cahun or
Halévy *Juive* reprieved from exegesis

—————

or language forming
texture, not explication—
gay arm dimple, magnolia
chalice-blossoms seen blurred

#15

*[imprisoned within Busby Berkeley
or the ethereal phlox]*

        I draw butt
well because butt is elementary

———————

we say nautical because
we want to avoid naughty

———————

imprecise speech stovepipes
our position and we come
to love the stove
and its scarred pedigree

———————

immoral penis is the obvious
place to juxtapose somno-
fascist and dewlap?
figuration and abstract bagel?

———————

is Tachisme a movement
celebrating rough clumsy
texture—why sigh again like
Ophelia or her supporters?

———————

dipping into Frigidaire
we praise the book and
know its contours are
orderly, governed by proxy
and whim in lower region

———————

the sick mental wife drops
glove, and law helps,
law is recourse
when stents bloom, if bloom
squeezes his daffodils
or the ethereal phlox

———————

he pretends to know my sex
and photos it—

———————

1940 is she ten and
reading *Black Beauty*
watching *Waterloo Bridge*
Vivien Leigh?

———————

1958 I'm reading
Marjorie Morningstar, sending
telegrams to Leigh's agent

———————

because syntax
has credibility and purse-like
we see syntax and can predict
its maneuvers and love
and forgive them in advance

———————

stones receive
sunlight, small
like teen friend dick-bush still
remembered

———————

lichen too has an unconscious—

———————

but his face
is so improbably handsome I
could die, his hair so phenomenal
I might need to do something radical—

———————

putting on lipstick
I wrote about fashion
classics in the Catskills

———————

he holds
himself like a hamburger,
hep to the hemisphere, an ass
presented to the camera
unconventionally

———————

Lauren Bacall
was Jewish and she died and I
really hope she doesn't

show up because that would hold
a certain amount of bliss
in its pocket

———————

    seersucker
yellow dream mother was
coherent, and the coherence fell
away like the difference
between ages 83 and 89—

———————

he treats me suddenly
with knife voice
edge shattering
Brünnhilde upon me

———————

    the leaf of
when she thought I was her
favorite son and I leaned
upon her knee or its in-
dentation like *A Star Is Born*
oceanic suicide

———

like a handsome guy in
basement doing laundry
and refusing to recognize me—

———

my mother's draught
of raw egg, raw beef
blood—to ease
the ache of being
a girl in that household

———

men were attracted to me
because of my big hips
she said

———

cup with Sudek facets—
specialize in simple
forms and render them clearly—

———

syntax contains only a few
available slots, capitalize
on each

———————

    I called
my mother and she resorted,
bless her, to polite formula

———————

the recourse was mah-jongg,
the caregivers were three

———————

he sees me as evil but has
no prosecutor with whom
to share his verdict—

———————

    it boils down to
a strange narcoleptic
cult of seriousness, to
be considered evil
by a quorum

———

a consciousness defined by
the status (washed, unwashed)
of a coffee pot or a
cock (cut, uncut)—

———

carving out a piece of
my *Nachtigall* stomach

———

    an eye imprisoned
within Busby Berkeley
corollas

———

    find
eros in blankness,
then behold his blotches—
don't cry, he survives his
blotches and neither splices
nor censors them—

#16

[a pear blue green slivered near brown]

the death books I haven't read

————————

my trumpet teacher is dead and I
don't want a lesson from his son,
a cougher

————————

"we are so alike"
my grandfather said
in his erotic inscription

————————

a recorded
clinical voice like silent
Nazimova's Salomé

————————

saying "data"
with a Frank O'Hara accent

———

the painting
has a frog in its throat

———

in the elevator mirror my
jaw looked swollen

———

at 13 she
sang in *Cavalleria Rusticana*—
debut dreamt or real?

———

I almost fainted
from imprudent diet pills

———

draw the grapes on his
arm—I want hair
to compose a proposal

———

begin to see any pelvis
as a covered wagon

———

and start to wonder how
genitals discern destination—
why each groin seems
to contain two genders

———

      to write in
the midst of a sexy demon-
stration on the subway

———

      wondering why the
man's knees are crossed,
legs and hands forming
a triangle like elongated Bruckner
phrase if Lenny Bernstein
were wearing a nightie

———

            we caress
on the street and I say
to the horse I am an
exhibitionist, not the black
glasses of Roman Polanski

———————

mouth of
a man who resembles
John Coplans

———————

perceiving
myself as a body by dis-
covering how to unearth
outlines beneath gesso,
digging a B pencil into
wet surfaces—

———————

he recommends a blending
brush, Richter's secret

———————

the year argyle
(sweater, socks)
tried to change
my life and failed

———————

he is praying,
not stroking himself—
the two activities in civic
space interchangeable

———————

clad legs signal the return
to a depressed world-view

———————

oil paint feels better when
it lands on top of oil paint
like brother-brother incest,
randy pallbearers

———————

Gandhi, Pavlova, Pavel
Tchelitchew, Paul Cadmus,
Bellini, which Bellini,
both Bellinis, the abstract
coven

———————

Jewish coven of
meddlesome Castevets
in *Rosemary's Baby*, seen
from Mia's paranoid
or perspicacious vantage

———————

to close my eyes and then
discover purple shoes
Hieronymus Bosch painted

———————

sickle moon a pear blue
green slivered near brown—

———————

adjectival
slot is where lust
can roost

———————

the world at 7:30 is
trepanned dusk
mitigated by pink

———————

lozenge pointillism, penis-ism
vs. pointillism—your points
are sticks or rods, like
saffron threads in plastic box
or like a sapphire
needle and the foam bed
the stylus rests its unworthy
napping head upon

#17

[diaper the diagram]

mother of
beheaded man says
nothing I can imagine

————————

aimed language
is destroyed language

————————

leg hair swirl,
leg alienation

————————

he says
shut up as if shut up
were charming

————————

the only
way to be excited

about life is to have
a sexual relation
with it

_____

      plaice under-
represented on menus

_____

         leave
grey lines evident
and muscular and willful,
allow yellow to become
an argument, different
yellows broken down
to appear vulpine

_____

      hairy balls
of a fifth-grade boy
are in memory piercing
yet underdeveloped—
a scrutinizing eye
shed on son's genitals

———————

Jayne Mansfield
shinier and quieter
has a right to feeble
lederhosen

———————

she
is on commode when I enter—
Delphic Oracle in love
with undone project

———————

he caresses mother
while I read *Sons and Lovers*
and note similarities 'tween
Cather and Lawrence
and wonder how they
rewrote their novels

———————

the red chair
I bought my mother
is broken

———

quote Winnicott and get dis-
respect for being too cerebral

———

stay human don't be post-human—
Tadzio's white suit a century ago

———

why do straight men
shout? some trans folk
also shout like Lana
Turner lookalike at Virgin
America gate

———

     I out-whine
my mother's paid companion

———

    apple in turd-
filled toilet we try to
flush, apple prevents
flushing—indelible dream
two years ago

————————

don't make uncomely
clunks with your bike lock

————————

flirt with my
Venezuelan grandfather
and fetishize his red hair
though he seemed not happy
to meet me

————————

please scream like
Phyllis played by Stanwyck
in *Double Indemnity* or
Berryman retching and pissing
in Iowa City

————————

she called
me sand crab and I
made much of my
subordination, I considered
my subordination literary

_____

       go backward and
diaper the diagram,
fossilize it, compote it

_____

       she kisses
me when I arrive though
we've never met before

_____

imagine asking father
to kiss his forearm, see
it vibrate

_____

walk down Wall Street
looking for a cheap watch
in 1984, like search
for naiad Moreau
(Gustave) tonsure smile

_____

Bellarmine is
my methodical brother's
alma mater

————————

the coordinating conjunction
insinuates or nullifies prophecy

————————

no snow,
no magnetism,
no gulag, no Zelda, no
criminal imagination

————————

smile when
you say my psychiatrist
died, smile whenever you
mention a friend's death,
invert the emotion

————————

my gall
arm too pale in

wattle crucifixion
self-portrait

_____

      brood and blame
are her signatures

_____

you like my ass? I of course
like your ass—calves trembling—
often calves tremble before orgasm
when standing in Prague
(Bel Ami) porn nursing home

_____

where upbeat music
and imminent death
inject you with vein-vial
of contradiction like Hannah
Arendt Marty Heidegger
fashion runway

#18

[a recipe for trick chicken]

a boy's slowly
watched rose bud, stalked
and stopped—

————————

trapped by perceived
reflection of his own charm,
wiggles his head but doesn't
think of budging

————————

she ate gift muffin avidly

————————

I picked up the two guys or
let them pick me up

————————

he asked where is this train
going and stood very close,

using his beauty
to blackmail me

———————

hustled to give him cuts
in line simply because
he looked like a young
Marcello Mastroianni

———————

      more of a turn-on
when there are many
"likes" attached to an image—
if 6,000 people "liked"
a naked photo I can imagine
their amassed desire

———————

        dark
house unlovely yew

———————

       mix
scarlet and white to create

dull orange circles inside
the figure—not
a figure, just a fetus-
style bulletin board

————————

Kafka's nude father in
"The Judgment" no
welcome mat to further
genital advances

————————

      barber-drudge
Puig-like sought me,
asymmetrical face
like a Shirley who stole
brother-virginity
(why is symmetry
beauty's sine qua non?)

————————

to redeem the hard-on
like a flash in nobody's
pan—

————————

concentrate on the
plot, mother

————————

I showed her
30 quickly-composed poems
and she liked the cousin
incest poem best because
it was short and horny
or at least modest and
without literary pretensions

————————

a night owl
depressed to become
the person he already is

————————

longing to
say *A Hussy in Gethsemane*,
longing to say *Vedanta!*
the movie musical or
Erwartung Vedanta!,
longing to say "furbelow"

———————

did you
know that Kandinsky and
Gabriele Münter were
lovers? even-keeled beak-face
of Wassily eating
modernism alive

———————

the squawking
quoit

———————

a quoit is a dolmen—
a tomb, not a bird

———————

a dolmen
squawking its burden
like a pet macaw
programmed to
perform epitaph

———————

in the days
when "department
store" had a ring
of maturity around it

———————

I'm a
sucker for a darkhaired
man with white pants,
however bruising or
incidental our intersection

———————

my baby brother
wanted to be an orchestra
conductor—

———————

he play-
conducted Mendelssohn's
violin concerto with a toy
baton leading imaginary orchestra
in orange-carpeted rumpus room
or somberly snapdragon

bedroom facing patio's
sodden dirty screens

———————

           I coached
his mock-tribunal

———————

Lucia di Lammermoor—as
if what mattered weren't
the madness but the
moor itself—

———————

the moor's the main
character, not Lucia,
but does she hammer
herself to enter the
moor (and drown)?

———————

      squatting
man lone on jetty
wore a boa

———————

did I
once have ringworm
in hippie bathroom?

———————

"Your father hated
your long hair" she
said but I couldn't
remember my father
having any opinion
whatsoever about my
hair or about any
other part of my
body or my bearing

———————

I mistakenly
thought my brother's
fifth-grade teacher (plaid
eminence) had some
mysterious connection to
Australia or New
Zealand and also

to his stuffed animal
Heffalump, not lovable
or articulate, a Rose Bowl
narcoleptic critter

————————

       bones
around heart's case
broken and then
fastened together again

————————

I could see the
broken spot—scar—
through her black dress's
opening

————————

I'm persecuted for
wiggling in my chair

————————

       exiled
from French classroom

I see the running
girl soil her white
stockings

———————

her name was Julie,
a pretty name, but after
I saw her accident,
Julie became a divided
name—half
ruined, half intact

———————

      I photographed
(with my Brownie) nextdoor
Cathy, the best of the
block's two Cathys—
the other Cathy had no
face I can remember

———————

a baby cried earlier and
now isn't crying

———————

Paul
Morel nearly beat up
his collier father, Paul
Morel passionately kissed
his mother, I was
overly nerdy in my
contractual stipulations

————————

the mayonnaisey
avocado sandwich she
derided though I'd
recommended it and dragged
her there to try it—
and then we fought in
front of aunt who
died thereafter

————————

clammy hands
after I walked ruminative
slow in white sneakers
past monarda—
sniffle-inducing dahlia

_____

and what is a
nasturtium, especially in
1913, what did nasturtiums
look like in 1913, the same
as now?

_____

ISIS beheaded a second
American

_____

my attentiveness
to contiguous relations (near,
beside, in the vicinity of)
is exaggerated or bite-sized

_____

like Dickinson's
eye operation

_____

back tooth
chipped on a plum pit

———————

rash
appeared Monday evening, noticed
after eating grapes

———————

"My Sharona" a song
we pretended to love because
it gave us straight cred

———————

handsome waist enters
Skid Row bathroom with
fuzz ear

———————

he looks
like corn on the cob,
swish Donald Duck—

———————

wanting
to remain orange and visible
though orange was never
within my capacity

———————

       "trick chicken,"
the chicken dish you
serve to tricks, mustard
chicken, a trick favorite,
any trick appreciates
mustard chicken—
here is the recipe

#19

[imaginary baby lunching on his own oblivion]

jury duty taught me
how to speak German

_____

write
to exorcise like Kafka
shutting his eyes—

_____

cum video
jammed—distrusted
size of jet

_____

down to 126 pounds,
two desserts at lunch—stopped drinking
temporarily

_____

diaspora from self began
when she borrowed my *Women in Love*
and wrote her notes on it but got
the professor's name wrong

—————

research my fetus and see if it's viable—
my theoretical fetus—

—————

dead person too has fetus,
is fetus

—————

Lenny Bruce, dead?
Leonard Cohen's
not dead

—————

two nipples is what we expect,
I found two nipples and was relieved

—————

Fido Dido t-shirt in spring I recall you
seeming to redeem cartoon attitudes
as revolt against early death from
named or unnamed disease

———————

I bought Raymond
Dragon t-shirts and shorts without
knowing that Raymond Dragon
was a porn star

———————

thread-voice montage—

———————

Chantal
Akerman taught at
City College

———————

stuck leaf
blocked by father liturgy

———————

like Joan Rivers in *The Swimmer*
with nude Burt Lancaster
or like when my father went into
raptures over Dante
at dinner, before
pesto, beyond abstraction
or Polk Street where S/M
was long-ago touchstone never
experienced but bear-posited—

————————

Polo cologne for boyfriend's birthday
though by then he'd transcended Polo—

————————

      my belief in continuous
motion versus his belief
in control and precision

————————

      why bother
is anyone's response to sibylline
labors and yet
I treasure unflaggingness

———

      study him, V
of shirt neck frozen there,
snapshot of his indifference
and tact

———

      the ocean floats
unsupervised as if the ocean
didn't have a mother

———

Vincent Price starred in three early
scary trashy movies I saw at
Fox Theater downtown, sleaze matinee
near smoke shop I could never enter
but now I see its visage—
mountainous smoke
shop more tangible than
the mind conjecturing you

———

      poached egg
on toast from mother

when I was sick, and I was
often sick—

_____

    that grass
too has its heft and weave

_____

    gigue and courante
memorized

_____

    to be inspired by nude
models in the room when
you write—

_____

posing nude in a kindergarten's
vicinity not illegal

_____

    people in the
U.S. never shut up—
take away either their
money or their loud voices—

————

"yes"
becomes her way to substitute
violin for Spinoza-scapegoating
on Baltimore train
platform where dead man
flashed VD penis at me—

————

if I can't say "her insane
arms," why keep a notebook?
—imaginary baby
lunching on his own oblivion

————

"two secretaries and four people"
she says—aren't secretaries people too?

————

he loved my
double but why didn't he realize
that I was the double, and give
me the voluptuous attentions
he gave my twin?

―――――――

we disapprove
of rhetoric but Duncan Smith
discovered voltage in
NORMA = NO ARM

―――――――

Norma
Desmond of *Sunset Boulevard*
according to Duncan Smith is
rhetorically missing an arm

―――――――

the Internet
is everybody's mother

―――――――

sideburn's agency meets
jaw's rebuttal

―――――――

like Eucharist
in anarchist mouth at thorn-
crown rest-stop diner

———

if his arms are cute and nude
he must be gay—voice is precise and
withholds aggression and so "is" gay—

———

      change gayness-oil,
dipstick to replenish or thwart
gayness because gayness
he told me is dead
like sacred library
text-fruit not
preserved before it spoils

#20

[thick book on mother-shelf pinnacled me o'er Tums]

good morning,
punctuated self—

————

Lee Krasner proves it—stay
awake to the redemptive glyph

————

scrutinized first chapter
and thought every statement dead wrong
except chartreuse and neon orange

————

cough
hurts right lung—even when I don't
cough, the right lung has a lumpy
vanilla crunch feeling—in my arteries too

————

M said *Faerie*
Queene is boring but thick book of it
on mother-shelf pinnacled me o'er
Tums—

———————

Hans Bellmer
receives hate mail USPS
grab bag of slain doll parts

———————

irenic
or oneiric gabbing
like 4-H club for gay hoofers
and Oona O'Neill
will be there and Nicole Kidman
good Nicole not bad Nicole
like moon Nicole versus Apollo Nicole—
but moon isn't *versus* Apollo

———————

what is the
Harlequin Romance equivalent of
"Friends, Romans, countrymen"?

————————

     obtuse
is an *ob* word like *obscene* or
oblate or *obsequy*—

————————

        to stretch
one's loins across the public domain—

————————

     why
do shrinks even when off-duty
refuse warmth and ebullience?
or do I specialize
in non-ebullient shrinks?

————————

use her talky head to block
the blinding sun

————————

tidbit was dead woman's word, we
shared *tidbit* and also *transcendent*
and now she's dead and I never told
her we shared *tidbit* and *transcendent*

———————

seeing *I Never
Sang for My Father* with my mother
long ago in a movie theater—

———————

be glad you never sang
for your father

———————

trying to prove that I
was Jewish despite ignorance
of the covenant—

———————

I saw a disgruntled
bride in flipflops lift her wedding dress
and walk at rush hour past Penn Station—

———————

stretched out like her dead
nurse mother whose
malted milk taste I still can't fathom

———————

mother whose car
we wrecked in stop-and-go traffic
en route to *Richard III* or *The Oresteia*

—————————

reaching
toward narrative but not necessarily
approving of the reach

—————————

which Kafka was I glad to meet
in Mykonos dream?

—————————

or a Massenet opera that might
not exist like *La Bouillabaisse*—
a long river cutting through *Manon*—
a good river advocating conversion
to frivolity—

—————————

reunion cakewalk for retiring
kindergarten teacher who
expresses recognition when seeing me—

———————

        rose glow
reflected on dull warehouse, blue
sky shined flat and pink by emigration
of rival color—

———————

sped up from pink extrojection,
wanting to subdue him in a scenario
of erotic torture based on my thinness
and his fatness—

———————

woman who ran a French
restaurant in St. Croix—
I envied her boozy
leathery ease—motorcycle—finality—

———————

writing on a paper napkin
a few un-causal enlightenment
nouns, like *junk, hazard,*
dumbness, Dillinger,
sexpot, dysfunction—

———————

     two hours of giddy
threshold consciousness—

———————

a few stunned lyrics
to *signalize* my stupor

———————

again the hilly outline's Pompeii
lump as the Jew hears it—
"the Jew" means not a
generality but a specific listener
who actually likes sex
and told me so

———————

     unless I'm this Jew, too,
doublecrossing the earlier,
spread-out, novel Jew—

———————

     stiff box for requested pearl
granted but lost, a pearl I didn't

understand though I craved it
as girl-sign under night-cover
of boy-dawn

———————

everyone has a nadir, a
Nadja—even Nadja has a Nadja

———————

   I spoke about
the solidity of nouns,
a U in the regarded
eggy or jizzy corner

———————

   my throat
is not my own, it has become
a colony of national interests

———————

   green soot posing
as lake cover

———————

            cream of spinach
soup, my mother's body when she suspected
food poisoning or experienced its greeny
symptoms—

          _____

          indiscreet
revelation about her ex—
I love triangulating
via unwise confessions

          _____

                    my lips
logical except when I teach
my baby sister the art of shoplifting—

          _____

Miltonic or Latinate relation to sideburn
length and thickness, George
Burns and Robert Burns and
Raymond Burr and Burl Ives—

          _____

                leave Burl
off the list of treasured burns

———

Blythe Danner isn't burly

———

        Morton Feldman
was once my mother's friend—
is that fact her property?

———

    we have in common
a predilection for killing plants—
no ability to keep a plant
alive—that's an exaggeration—
three roses in her sideyard, maybe more

———

    Carlota my unmet
unphotographed step-grandmother,
to designate her with regal sobriquet

———

another green succulent
covering a pond
surface with scum

———

skim the nitwit
coating off my tongue

———

Thoreau died at 44,
killed by Apollo

———

you have to be killed
by someone, might as well
be killed by Apollo

#21

[the old soiled carpet of the wish to be Anaïs]

writing on the bruised
body and seeing into the
bruise's locked backyard, not
psychoanalyzing the incursion
but appreciating its scissory
up and down

———————

remembering the wish
to be Anaïs Nin—

———————

stepping on the old soiled
carpet of the wish to be Anaïs—

———————

liking
the pullulation of scratch marks
and their glistering anonymity

———————

florid
British perfume wrongly purchased
for stepfather—the perfume stank
so why did I buy it?

—————

     the entire sky
with a palette knife is scratched
turquoise opal—
no underlying tint to betray it

—————

a sick tint inundating the marsh

—————

I celebrate mother's sunset
or I am cloud making her
sunset more inspiringly Turneresque—

—————

to scratch through the page until
it dies, and no credit given
to the scratcher

—————

desecrating or seeding
the maternal potty

_____

tinkle the "retrieved"
philosophical void/fold

_____

Senta's glamorous orgasm
at spinning wheel

_____

    to observe poop
is Beethoven-like, a Kreutzer voyeurism
vis-à-vis poop's supremacy

_____

    summer
mononucleosis-emulating
naps during Schumann's
"Spring" Symphony

_____

pan-sheet pizza as
counterpoint to squeezing
junior-high lunch-monitor's
"boobs" in shiny polyester dress

————————

a farm lies inside your eyes,
you want to pee to see if the
farm exists, you think
"existence" is negligible but
you want to pay lip-service
to Being, Dad invented it, you
respect (or fear) Dad's thunderous
inventions—making him marble
sorghum or sphagnum
coating a forest dangerous
in itself but not when razed

————————

bite stranger's upper arms, triceps,
fat around triceps—
bite rocky bridge of nose,
bite back of neck, bite

love handles, bite
stomach and calves
of lacustrine
youth, a Pan or Actaeon—bite
forearms, chew them but
without teeth

————————

    stamp Beatrice on his
stomach, Beatrice tattoo on
calf muscle—shave hair so
Beatrice is visible

————————

       dead
father stands aloof in mausoleum
of stamp-collecting and
signing Rembrandts falsely,
Dürers, Schieles and Giacomettis—
I bit them too

————————

    stoop I sat on waiting
for three o'clock so I could be

admitted to house through garage
door, cold dark garage with father's
books on feeble shelves—

———————

     stepfather's
books also later kept in garage—
husbands are garage material—

———————

     not always
true, *Saint Genet* was inside,
Psychopathia Sexualis was inside—
Vedanta was inside

———————

as was my longing to bite
his trapezius muscles,
their October overhang, a
denial tribute rhythmic and
regarded—

———————

she mocked hips
of jeans-wearing poet—
I admired the poems but she
disparaged the hips

———————

was she jealous
of the poems? were the hips mocked
or the pants, the belt, the overall
severity of habiliments?

———————

nor were my mother's parents thoroughly
interested in me—why pretend?

———————

Rose Kennedy didn't love every
Kennedy equally, nor did Joe—
we choose our favorite Kennedy
and then ignore the others

———————

father tried
to make baby sister smile

for the visiting photographer—
she cried, ignoring
her chance to be a child star—

---

as if *elle*
and *il* were definite articles
rather than fidgety pronouns—

---

mother smiles
when she says that someone
died—death is weird so she smiles

---

also she smiled when we saw *Prime
of Miss Jean Brodie* at drive-in
and a woman's naked breasts
appeared on juvie-screen

---

milkshake
smile because the boys are seeing
a woman's breasts on film for the
first time, father too in car

———

she smiles at me and
brother but not at father—

———

68th Street—bang!
Hojotoho! sunny 67th—

———

tongue I want
to draw and almost drew
but then squelched the impulse

#22

[daisies differed from violet gentians]

pop song I heard in Tokyo
movie theater, 1974—

———————

perky Annette
Funicello-style vocalist, knowing
she'll soon be bruised and forgotten

———————

tried to tell erudite
faun my "Ella
mi fu rapita" (*Rigoletto*) epiphany

———————

"Ella mi fu rapita," she
ravished me, she crowds
my consciousness, my men
kidnapped her but I don't yet
know about the kidnapping,
first her beauty kidnapped me

————————

precision
reminds me of clover, bluebells,
chlamydia, Tommy Lee
Jones, James Earl Jones,
auto-erotic suicide

————————

when
I accompanied her *Sanglots*

————————

I told him
who Lily Pons was—
mentioned Ponds cold cream—
also Attis, self-mutilator

————————

woman waiting for a van
had only two or three
fingers per hand

————————

skittishness and avoidance of eye
contact make her impossible to
locate, a puffy cloud, foam
instead of filet mignon

———————

mother's body on 9-20-58
is aperture I peered out
(nothingness, my
first home) into the glaring
world—every September 20th
I return to the aperture

———————

and I have no other aperture

———————

      Williamsburg's
German Earth oil
paint, not really
German, headed
toward moonstone

———————

she called a caregiver
a tramp and created a ruckus

———————

birthday father stood
in structure overlooking
ocean's mysterium

———————

pestering him for a subscription
to *Modern Photography*—"are
you interested in photography?"
was his reasonable reply

———————

did he understand
I wanted nudes, a subject
twinned to photography?

———————

brought deep indigo painting
home, kissed its canvas sides—
fingers rubbed nubs

———————

discover a hole, discard
sock—sound of wasted not-darned
self falling in garbage
can is disgusting

————

Sei Shōnagon distinguishes
between delightful and disgusting things

————

      my finger
(or my nose's inside lining)
smelled of dog shit

————

bank lobby smelled, too—
crap tracks on heat-
wave carpet

————

Robert Creeley showgirl
like Robert Goulet *Showboat*

————

or Liza too, one decade (1960s)
containing both her rise
to eminence and a perilous
paperback (*Christy*) which I
misremember as a book
about a Swedish paraplegic—

———————

why was *Christy* perennially
on sale through Scholastic
Book Club?

———————

          a brother's
cock (it fits
into a copper vase) is embodied
ink of overstimulation

———————

          a boy can
be a woman's mother

———————

          dreamt I
said to an administrator at

The New School, "Don't you feel
compromised by your desk's
nearness to the toilet?"

———————

      limit myself to zinnia's fine
decisive lines, understand
floral rhetoric I need to
dwell within

———————

      imagine
an aristocratic (Nancy
Mitford) face powder
named *poudre de l'héritage*

———————

      I wrote her travail
down

———————

I knew daisies differed
from violet gentians—

———————

gentian violet dye
to prevent VD in WWI

———————

      gentian violet
stains any skin, including
mine, awaiting crystal

———————

now I must navigate
around the stains and pretend
every splotch increases sapience

#23

[to refuse the sick home's lure]

listened to 83-year-old Magda
Olivero in Milan sing
"Sola, perduta, abbandonata" *Manon
Lescaut*—convincing steady tone

———————   .

      Actaeon hit me, hit
me hard, Actaeon
perched on my nothingness

———————

      returning to
Baltimore, first time since 1981—
seeing stoops when train first
reached humid outskirts

———————

picked up gay
underground newspaper,
visited The Hippo

———————

bald Tomás
wrist in hot tub, saw
dick float down there—was
I also floating my in-
admissible dick?

———————

call
me Public Enema

———————

Patsy Kelly saying "Trenton
New Jersey" in *No, No, Nanette*

———————

pursue
elegance and then drop it
like a memory
"basket" in the Caravaggio
Bacchus sense

———————

in little brother's
abandoned bedroom
she blew me as
charity or to settle a score

———————

sense memory
on tongue of where
a clitoris is
on the mother-knitted afghan,
pool beneath us,
her moisture not mine—
later the fever-sweated sheets

———————

refuses to let him come
home on weekends even
though he's miserable and homesick

———————

why is he homesick for
a sick home?—to refuse
the sick home's lure—

———————

The Hippo
down the street from 15
East Eager, front window
smashed, mailbox awry,
narrow doorway

———————

visit her in Truro,
mushroom-hunting pregnant
woman in tic-tac-toe socks,
mouth pucker from Aspergum

———————

for nine months my father
paid my rent, $150

———————

did Odysseus pay
rent for Telemachus?

———————

dream about
bully who wanted to knife me

———————

bully who invaded
our house wrote a knitted
(sewn?) art book

—————————

      after recovering
from wanting to knife me,
he asked me to read
his manuscript—he hung
on my verdict

—————————

I read the book silently,
reserving judgment

—————————

the bully changed
clothes so he could
dance with old ladies
at summer mansion cotillion

—————————

the elevator smells of a
raccoon she said, but

when the man got
off the elevator it stopped
smelling like a raccoon

_____

the bully had a huge
hard-on I was
overeager to touch

_____

laughing Lear and his potty
daughters

_____

piebald moon's
sound waves simulate words
rising from unruled
(chthonic?) prelinguistic pit

_____

harvest
from the pit and not the agora

_____

mistaking Haussmannization
for Housmanization as in
A. E. Housman *Shropshire Lad*

————————

    not three
words in English to describe
his escape from North Korea

————————

    third-grade school
library stillness, Edward
Eager *Half Magic*—
magically for one year in
Baltimore I lived on East
Eager Street—

————————

for Kandinsky-smitten
1981 I write quickly now
a *Strauss* (bouquet) of tribute—

————————

    I knew a Yolanda
once but who was she?

what was her claim on
the universe? a Yolanda
claim, fugal yet clarion

————————

horizon begs shine
from her tilted sublime shoe

————————

five blocks north of us
the houses held angular
wounded violinists
and the rumored girl
with webbed fingers

————————

        starting four
times to elucidate Hades
and giving up because
Hades (my future home)
can't be elucidated—

#24

*[to slow down his mouth,
a clear theology of phlegm]*

bought porn mag overpriced
in South End—false
fire alarm rousing me
from the disappointing hotel

———————

Rumpelstiltskin
the first play I went to,
first opera an abridged
Hansel and Gretel

———————

I beat the shit out of
Hansel said Gretel

———————

clemency for
the bitter French teacher
and her hard conjugations

———————

*I Remember
Yiddishe Mama*, a
grumpy first-nighter in Warsaw
before grumpiness stressed
out the shapely
cat, X-rated

—————

Prince Hal's renunciation and
Walter Benjamin's renunciation
the wrinkles that make
physiognomy red and
revolutionary, hierarchical
Pharaohs leading my
people downward

—————

distressed munchkin, you
didn't grow—

—————

I waited for the famed
growth spurt—

—————

stinky cruising
in Westport toilet—
a glory hole so
huge it wasn't really
a hole—it was a major
defeat of the wall

————————

nude man carrying gun
nighttime near conservatory obelisk

————————

my game was to slow
down his mouth and then
delete it, hirsute
daybed with cologne
half-nelson

————————

little boy with gay
father in Amsterdam
wheelchair

————————

only happy when
I'm discussing rump—
giggles come from opiated
outer space

————————

no longer hug writer vocation
nervously—discard vocation,
shirk or spurn it, then
return to cracked,
crumpled vocation, say hello
to its bruises

————————

or just crush Deneuve
petals, imagine them
now parfum a phone
number version of a switched-on
Deneuve, Deneuve simply
what William James
called a perching

————————

her fits were aporetic—
define aporetic pleez—
and also irenic

_____

Dalton Trumbo
leglessness and cocklessness,
waking dismembered

_____

a cheap sinny
voice, "sinny" means
skinny + Pliny,
like Pliny who wrote
about Mount Vesuvius
erupting? or Musée Carnavalet
showcasing Proust's brass bed?

_____

I'm not a
storyteller—accept
Céline filth identity, cilia
of our filth a draped
serrure, a car's child lock

————

          make it
a dialogue between two
wounds, car crashes, the devout
and the simpleton—squash
the simpleton by sitting
on his face

————

no wonder your son is
acting out in class,
and then you say Rosh
Hashanah and loudly
cackle and freak out

————

        henceforth a
life devoted to obscenity
as release from Babel
or strangehold of imaginary
"law of the mother," a
chapter Lacan forgot to write

————

"tit" in his crude
mouth obsessed with
powers of syllable
"tit" as molecular
agent of language—
"tit" palindrome sets off
language as a bad
mood sets off an angry
mouth—

————————

he tried to
sexually harass me
with a Jeb Bush or Oliver North
mask appended to his
ass as he thorped me—
"thorped" is thoroughly
porked + herpes-provender

————————

a diagnostic moment for
Shilly—"Shilly" is
Lili Marleen + Shirley

Temple (the drink) and
macadam also pretending
to be macaroon—

—————

sneezing
without a clear theology
of phlegm

—————

nearness to
Bouvier but forgiven Bouvier
not the imperious version—

—————

in dream, kissed her full
pouty lips, Catholic Mass
in progress—

—————

she said "I take
the Mass seriously"—
I silently agreed
to swallow her Mass—

----

       reading about South
Boston busing in 1975 before
college, not understanding
Boston except as a cloud of buses

----

did I dream last night
of Longy School of Music's
stone house and my mother's
friend studying there
in 1950 and my *Valses*
nobles et sentimentales
ham-handed in 1977?

----

      someone
decapitated a co-worker
in a factory—describe
rage of a fired worker

Joyce Carol Oates *Zombie*—
tell my mother's father

I'm reading *Childwold* and
not sure if he's impressed

———————

Buffalo when I was 20
years old Albright-Knox
museum Jackson Pollock
defamiliarization
snow and country club—
unable to chat tennis golf
or stockbroking—

———————

the privilege of dying among
her books is gone—
library stored, dispersed

———————

first babysitter Gail across
the street cocoa mouth savor
or more educational, like saffron

———————

in dream
did it signify maturation
or deliquescence that my
paints splattered and I no
longer kept them neatly
pooled on palettes?

#25

[the meat she chose and folded]

    reading only a few
paragraphs of *Silent
Spring* and quickly deciding
it's my Bible, life now
defined by *Silent Spring*
B.C./A.D.

————————

    also *Panic in Needle
Park*, library book
read on a bunk
bed, a dark cabin
during the day, where?

————————

"graham cracker" screams
tot with damaged
voice, crackly and
Garland though only one
year two months old

---

saying Martha Graham
when he means
graham cracker

---

she sucked him off for free
and was not yet fully
famous—to suck off
Elliott Gould while not
yet fully famous!

---

did mother's vagina
have a special smell?
I bet she douched
with extra care

---

dreamt of leaves
on backyard rocks
as punishment exhibit—
trying to re-experience
leaves fallen disorderly

on lava rocks and to
remember sensation (horrid)
of fingers sieving leaves
from lava

————————

  engorged
time while probing
rocks for hidden
skunk leaves—learning
to hate the leaves I gather

————————

mud in front yard,
seeing mud, knowing
I might need to eat
mud even if her
statement ("eat mud")
was hyperbolic and
rhetorical

————————

  before
a job interview, I see
top of his ass declivity

_____

I say "you know there's
a relation between noun
and thing, and eventually
noun replaces thing"

_____

butt in green
army pants, grey under-
wear strap showing—

_____

he
tooth-scorned Jung—
Freud too made an appear-
ance in dog terms

_____

f-stop of his
serial anus or
just its back
lawn, dry, unwatered

_____

the meat
she chose and folded
and refrigerated, a knack
for cold cuts

———————

burnt Vietnam war
journalist face—
blond historian with
prosthetic leg,
anchorite stays to jerk
him off

———————

block lady Meredith's
blurry cross-eyes in
butterfly glasses
like Todi hilltown
sunrise birdflock—

———————

why didn't Meredith,
barefoot in muumuu, speak?

why did Meredith's son
bully me and make me strip?

———————

      choose
abstraction, relax
the figure's grip—
goodbye to individual
nudes, they paralyze

———————

Liszt's birth
out the head of
Mendelssohn and Meyerbeer,
a Socratic (buttfucked)
relation to Meyerbeer—

———————

Ravenswood Lucia's
marmalade smile, "wedgie"
minimalism nightmare
not hers but mine

———————

also Eve Harrington
an Elektra, a deviously
mimetic German
upstart spiraling

———————

Lotte Lenya isn't Lot,
isn't salt

———————

     we danced
straw-gold Rumpelstiltskin
jig—like a riddle
("where's the hidden cock?")
sung by a cuckoo

———————

     decide to narrate
Nuremberg in the voice
of Peter Altenberg circa 1900—

———————

     if the drive
past college joggers can

be trusted in 1970,
hypothesize *college gym*
as voyeur paradise

———————

in dream practicing
Fantasiestücke "Des Abends"
evening this time the
passage rhythmically broken
down—when a listener
questions my morseling
method I defend it as prank
and security

———————

     toward middle of
"Des Abends" second page
the babysitter said the
untimely babysitter said
the measure fails and the line
becomes rhapsodic,
unmeasured, no more
bar lines, and yet the motive
is rational

———————

you could imagine
bar lines, hallucinate them,
but even that strategy fails

#26

[carpet nubs always a lady treehouse]

with barking
larynx, mature dwarf in
dream walked
by grocery—a "quit" (cute) kid,
his hair a male chignon
pinned up, balletic

_____

the more unpalatable
he looks, the harder
I get as reflex

_____

choosing private brain
cathedral for erotic
ceremonies possibly a
huge mistake

_____

says he castrated
himself in front of undergraduates

———————

dead pet turtles starved
dry aswim in fecal
pond of my cruel making

———————

father put goldfish in
toilet while he cleaned
their bowl—did one
goldfish swim
down sewage
tunnel and disappear
from our careful house?

———————

a tomato door onto nothingness
the errant goldfish took,
choosing toilet hole as
blocky entrance

———————

"blocky"
means unlocked +
bewildering + Bloch

the composer of *Schelomo*—
a Yom Kippur goldfish
repenting for what? for eye
contact with its master-creator?

––––––––––

Adam and Eve
not allowed eye contact
with suspicious
obsessive God

––––––––––

I can picture
Eden, a dumbshow garden

––––––––––

he wanders in shorts
through Beethoven bagatelles—

––––––––––

Vienna Secession leg hair, more
in middle than on edge,
signifies smartness and shyness

––––––––––

uncut and creative, alone
with math and Poppa—
Where's Poppa? George Segal

———————

I resemble Horshack
not the Fonz—or is
Horshack the same
as Sunday school?

———————

      the drooling
kid who talked too much,
a sassy redhead, not
red hair but red mouth,
Los Gatos suntan
wealth? or lubrication

———————

so he slid down Poppa, slid
past measure, and Long
Islanded upward to
a different, cruel Poppa,
Kafka-pupa, depending
where you put the crack

and the lieder, Esterházy
torte and maidenhair

————————

boys should bathe, a
boy who doesn't bathe
is a sinner

————————

William-Carlos-Williams-influenced
arm hair isn't an offense—
it's clean, withheld, monolingual

————————

boy smell
communicates unlove—
and that's why we disdain
boy smell, a Rhine

————————

S/M chaps,
no underwear, the room
smells of leather
intelligent bisexual urine

————————

arm hair in
abeyance, Celan, not
Celan, deciding to learn
German the night I'm
abandoned, flocking to
"he spurned me" myth
for dove purposes

———————

he whispers
"darker purposes" in
effaced memory tunnel

———————

go to sleep little smelly
bunny, flick on your
aversive puppy-mind

———————

do you
dislike being near boys?
their loud unkempt
pimply horizontality

———————

lick my lips visibly to
signal alliance with *Swan Lake*

———————

beard-smell turnstile refusing
effete guy with loose shorts

———————

luxe clim, "clim"
is climate ruined,
also clinamen as forked
interpretive turn

———————

stomach in side
view as he raised himself—
my hardness is logical
response, as if hardness
established tribute and
connection to espied guy

———————

I've depucelated him
optically, sure bet

is optical depucelation,
a novel of optical
depucelation is magical
thinking light show

———————

colored gels of wish
and distorted psychoanalysis
for severely troubled linguists

———————

of Browning's
"Last Duchess" I forgot to
speak—ask them what
full measure taken
means and mention salience
of "Last Duchess" as
dramatic monologue
enacting possession
of ventriloquy-matrix—

———————

voice-box held in
pincers of novelistic
crenellation

————

when
Henry James holds
the forceps and your
skull suffers as a result

————

low
not Bacall but the voice
rides on top of a net
and the net frightens us,
sister jumps on net and
I ride syllable-horse

————

pregnancy 8mm snippet
of gay guy spelunking
in mock gorge

————

spinning wheel of Gretchen
pregnant already

————

I see a womby treehouse,
stern womb-traveler between
world wars

———————

      admiration of Robin
Williams before suicide,
the unexplained anagram

———————

I can't help my
clumpiness, noun-clump
rather than clarity

———————

knee pathos because of
mother's photographed
or remembered tartan knee—

———————

tartan was her skirt,
never tartan
were her pants

———————

   pants rode high
above ankles, thin vista
spoken of and therefore
now forbidden—my
twig property

———————

like a treehouse
her ankles, a low
treehouse above
carpet nubs—carpet
nubs always a
lady treehouse—

#27

[a smelly Him we saluted by
saying or eating Port Salut]

Gwyneth Paltrow compli-
mented my jacket—
this isn't a dream—

_____

we crossed
paths on a theater
staircase—she said
"I love your jacket"

_____

sing "A" four
times with husky monotone

_____

three idiosyncratic hairs
in arm crook—
I thought they were
error squiggles

————

Tante Alice's favorite
cheese was Port Salut—

————

      was Port
Salut a seaport,
like Port Washington?
was Port Salut a way
of treasuring the other
by saluting it, or Him?
maybe Salut was Him,
and we saluted Him by
saying Port Salut—
a smelly Him
we saluted by saying
or eating Port Salut

————

      he rejects me
like a dead body
rejecting air and earth—

————

wanted to
suck his elbow,
write a review of his elbow

———————

Ionic volute
hair thrice paranoid
reassessed in theater bathroom

———————

sing Strauss
and then die, sing
unmonumental Bellini
song perfectly and
die unvisited

———————

on the verge of fainting
before opening night
curtain rises

———————

inebriate
rediscovery of *rubato*

live Moffo "Amami,
Alfredo" opposite Domingo,
1970—

—————

     Dickinson
said Domingo in
a phrase I misremember
as "finer than
Domingo" or "a Domingo
never brewed"

—————

     they laugh
at the space between my legs

—————

Widener Library named
after a drowned son

—————

books intersect
with drowning because
Prospero drowns his book

———————

did D. H. Lawrence
write drowned books?

———————

      Ginsberg capsule, his
art in a pill box,
memory crumbs in 24-hour
slow-dose

———————

restaurateur at the Center
for Queer Happiness
I serve buckwheat batter
existentialism *assoluta*

———————

she cut up her book in
a Reuben sandwich
club formation

———————

scholarly quiet man
hadn't shaved in two days—

stubble-darkened face
contrasting with light-
colored shoes turned him
into my art piece or
art *tout court*

—————

stubble envy
began with the Big Bang

—————

gay boys in sleazy harbor-
bar picked me up for
gender-and-poetry Marxist-
anarchist lessons but after
a few minutes of considering me
the central attraction they lost
interest and began deriding

—————

strung-out odalisque,
hipster continuo on bed

—————

cruel gay wine
bar in Villefranche-sur-Brooklyn,
an angry male
proprietor, blankness where
I expected a maître d'

―――――――

committed to phrenology's afterlife,
taking obscene photos of isolated
sentences

―――――――

he played an unlikable
character with bushy beard

―――――――

after the movie
I told him "You're much
handsomer in person"

―――――――

but he was not my Sanka-
overdosing logician

―――――――

somebody nun-like
blessed the pus and
flattered it

————————

just bite his elbow and be
done with it, even if I fail
the team and am accused
of being indelicate

#28

[douched by my own hieroglyph]

I wiggle and sigh too
frequently, it must
distract my German
neighbor

_____

hair
on back of neck,
can't figure out
whether hair begins
under the shirt

_____

find
bodywork book that shook
Charles Olson—ask unshaven
German stranger why he
is taking notes on theosophy

_____

throat covered with
indecipherable
stubble implies con-
tinuity, nothing to
obstruct bliss

_____

rebbe
with louche sagging eyes

_____

try an "h" word
(like "horticulture") to escape
my scapegoating impulse

_____

without a dictionary
slowly translate
an impossible poet

_____

read
Wittgenstein's horoscope or
treat *Investigations* as my

faultless horoscope—what
was Wittgenstein's sign?

————————

dreamt no one liked
my mother or at first
didn't like her but then after
the substitute teacher liked her
the unruly class had to admit
mother's Minerva-smartness

————————

I couldn't read her
likeability—she was block
bold italics lost in
the margin, a *Lear* distillate

————————

I like short men I
told the psychoanalyst, also
told her that bathrooms
were my churches—
seeking large public

lavatories with no clientele
so I can relax in privacy

———————

Old Spice after-
shave as Xmas gift for
father in 1965, a good year
for Old Spice

———————

masseur
had ambiguous roommate
with semi-religious credo—
scattered and incomprehensible

———————

and I wanted bear more than
I wanted my own adult life

———————

her shrink is dead so no
one can provide non-
sensical baby food

———————

           my plaid shirt
too tight but at least
I weighed only 123.5 pounds
last night

———————

brought obscene ("beat-sheet")
Guyotat for inspirational reading

———————

           choose a big book
to translate weirdly, without
fealty, and call my version
Crock Baud or
Bawdy Crock

———————

           crock is opium,
so crock pot is when you
smoke pot while
ingesting opium and your
brain has an "innie" orgasm

———————

when you're in
a dismal state a cello
concert in a church seems
like a royal wedding

—————

when my mother turned 40
she bought a bike
and began riding
around the neighborhood,
usually by herself—

—————

can't picture
father on a bike—
he didn't dilly-dally
with unfocused pursuits

—————

in love with rectilinear
theorist's thick nose,
stunted speech, cockiness
held back by stunt—"stunt"

is to be so stunted you
are a carnival, one body
encapsulating elephant and trapeze

———————

his nipples
promised cream
soda and celery tonic

———————

rich man adopts
brain-damaged teen and turns
him into poetic genius
only three people appreciate

———————

when I pause I
am Gertrude in *Hamlet*

———————

malted milk drunk by
Horatio at soda fountain

———————

falling into
pigsty while we watch
Wizard of Oz by daylight
and are rewarded for it
by restored Jitterbug number,
Jitterbug cut and kept
in cave-dark hypothalamic archive

_____

inadmissible prick's
outline behind blurry glass
pane in a photograph he's not
shy about posting

_____

I see it
and he knows I see it or
potentially any of his
colleagues can see it

_____

line
up four square panels
and then drip simultaneously

on all, with unforewarned
motion—don't aim for circles

———————

home is Ava Gardner
rescinding me and she isn't
Ava, just dark eyes
in a magazine

———————

please use a
special rune soap—
I am douched
by my own hieroglyph

———————

Lon Chaney
discovering sums like
Oscar Wilde's wife,
no pension for sodomite's
wife precious and few are
a sodomite's wives in
Karen Carpenter's feeding
tube

—————

we meet at subway and
she looks at me harshly
because once I climbed
on top of her

—————

            theses
of Luther pinned to toilet
stall door?

—————

was she in Auschwitz
brothel? so my mother said—
another cousin lost twins
in Theresienstadt

—————

            met tall
swarthy Sontag type, rushed,
abstract, in fog-wrapped
recognition scene

—————

                investigate
my "mental weather" (her
phrase) and also
tempests not my own

　　　————

to be fond of corpses or
comfortable with corpses

　　　————

                find
book about Israeli Jew
who renounced Judaism

　　　————

                un-
focused investigation is still
investigation—

#29

[libel is the only way to keep a voice limber]

high boy voice is girl-like
saying *indifference* in cahoots
with not stopping
because only prudence
ever made me stop

———————

sopping braggart top
seven inches and no interest
in reciprocating

———————

stop caressing his breasts
in public

———————

touching a dying man's
nipples can be instructive

———————

old bladders
frighten me though they
are mine

———————

so many men waiting in line to
pee, varieties of length,
bouncin' men, all lambent

———————

avoiding Christ
compositional matrices and
stumbling past self-created
grids

———————

reconstruct
mother's kindergarten fling

———————

the interviewer said "a voice
of liquid gold" and made
the soprano repeat the canned
phrase as if she'd coined it

———————

        Giovanna
d'Arco while I gradually
mix permanent lemon, Mars
violet, peony red, and zinc
white to make a German late-
style grey

———————

       slowed-down breasts
in solitaire haze, belly
of man serving me deli

———————

don't turn prisoners
into tourist attractions

———————

       certainty on top
of certainty, humping
certainty like Imelda
Marcos humping her shoes

———————

if I'm an investigator accept
the strictures of investigation

———————

dreamt sister
said "puss" and was held
within my father's gaze as
"Puss in Boots," emblematic
fairy tale of teething and
favoritism

———————

should I read
Dr. Spock to learn about
my own colic and the
world's colic?

———————

take Beckett's heirs
to see a hausfrau *Godzilla*

———————

boi grrl, wave
to Hanoi despite American
culpability unforgiven

———————

dream—Tante Alice
incontinent, my mother
says something to Alice
about the "slaughterhouse,"
that would be preferable to
shitting oneself, or else Alice
becomes such a burden
that my mother sends her
to the slaughterhouse—

———————

Alice sits patiently
with messy drawers
at dinner table but finally
complains or cries and
demands to be changed—
I realize that my father is
the only one with the strength
and commitment to change her,
but it will be traumatic for him
to see her buttocks and genitals
because she is his dead
mother's sister—

———————

Alice is
taking a night course and
we notice that her conversation
as a result has grown
scintillating, though my
father says that she
still crudely thinks
in terms of celebrities,
a limiting optic—

———————

I need to intrude
my own body between
oncoming car and baby
to save its life and thereby
forfeit my own

———————

couple Guyotat's
Coma and Arendt's
Origins of Totalitarianism

———————

disgust creates a frame
for eroticism

———————

      Beckett describes
a mouth trying to shit
its tongue

———————

WOODY:
BARBRA:
Scene 1, Scene 10,
Scene 30, Scene Anything—
write 100 Scenes for
Woody and Barbra, *A*
Novel in 100 Scenes

———————

      libel is the only
way to keep a voice limber

———————

glossolalia and echolalia
praised and claimed, I
am gloss and echo

———————

not interested in
my body except my nipples
verbally, large white
Jello 1-2-3 ass aloft

————————

hey Mom it's me, she says,
knocking on bathroom door

————————

focus group pink lust
for boy thigh in novel
or in lisp *récit*

————————

short
fourth-grade teacher Mrs. Nigh
sick for one semester—
what was her illness?

————————

it was an Austin-Healey
Mormon-illuminated nightly
homo-theater, Alexander

the Great what? Great
Hemorrhoid? and other tales
like *Jaws* of woe, splice
pudding, jail butt

———————

stipple on Blitz cud

———————

       becoming depraved and
therefore incapable of psycho-
analysis, too much pre-
cum for *Durcharbeitung*
Working-through

———————

             flayed
repeatedly for rebuff
Golgotha, a tidy X
on his udder

———————

      I create for
him an udder, I have

the strength to create
for Jesus-father a portable
udder

———————

in dumbfounded *Potemkin*
brain, small truck wreck
almost kills scholar

———————

his legs and trapezius press
against grey cords and tan
shirt, easy-lay James
Taylor encasing Joni
hard-on devout missal,
Monkees Wizard of Oz
hybrid gefilte Oz, like
Tin Man Micky Dolenz

———————

a nod to "Land of Nod"
Stevenson poem, anthology
lordly on shelf

————————

           skid
between meanings, allusions,
episodes, quickness scatter-
seed

————————

Celan pronounced like Hush
Puppies or Glenn Close
Fatal Attraction Malipiero?
or maledizione moment in
Rigoletto as whore antidote
to sympathy-burst for
sister of Sparafucile slayer
headed toward *True
Detective* or Tante
pillage

————————

in hemlock-society guerdon,
a typical blot in
life's book Anna Karenina
is reading

---

deviation a subset
of interruption—no, interruption
a subset of full stop

#30

[a burning bush on the brain]

man skeptical
of my philosophical death orientation
as all men are skeptical

_____

drew apple in two stages
of decomposition

_____

I've heard of
banality of evil he says
sarcastically

_____

claim whoredom as
literature's origin, castrated
Origen

_____

foul apiary
where Origen gets laid, sinks
fangs into Lethe, or
webcams Lethe

—————————

mother's "crazy" logo
and my theft of it

—————————

if Artaud were
mother and she had golf bags
or was bully to golf team

—————————

another spiralcurled Peter
to be ignored by, his Christ
muscles flashing

—————————

need sandpaper because
gesso is too shiny and lacks
tactility

———————

wiggly
butt walking between steam
bouts welcomes intruder,
accepts syntax's finger

———————

the house or my body in the
house can't endure the experience
of being wrongly hailed

———————

how can
I choose to become not-me?

———————

watched him
give a desultory blow job

———————

babies need a body wall
to lean against

———————

purple dried hydrangea in polished
silver vase was part of my
thematically lucid phase

————————

Rudy
Burckhardt committed suicide,
so did his lover Edwin Denby—

————————

Agamben refuses
fingerprinting

————————

is it wrong
to imitate Miró? remember
King James, he wrote
a good Bible

————————

in junior high
a kid who shaved and
had sideburns plagued
(not played) an instrument

————————

         crack
open her movements and find
latent percussiveness

————————

I touched the bird doctor's
mustache

————————

      he itched
his balls while he served me,
then said sorry
and debrided my sunflower

————————

         discovering
how to draw without making
the observed object a punishing
judge

————————

      the object needn't be
reproduced, but it must provide
concrete lines and curves to mimic

———————

optic fairy
berries in a pond
riot

———————

his show-off
ochre crack, ecclesiastical

———————

Beaumont and Fletcher and my
arty studiousness in beach
town tropic window left open
to panic on Ellis Island

———————

who will buy
my Oliver Twist
sexual abuse mess
hall grub rehash?

———————

I tried to
describe my ice cream man

to him but he was still high
from crystal meth

———————

twice wrongly described
myself as clairvoyant

———————

       explain
why strangers are
soothing, why sparrows
are a lowly bird, why
genitals—touchy
and spotty—top
the hierarchy

———————

let Barbra
or Woody
be the investigator
asking these questions

———————

       make
love with a fungus, respond to

gay men by fetishizing fungi,
my fungus infection and yours,
their combined folly

———————

we start
our theory of West Coast
"cool" montage with *Taxi
zum klo*—jump cut
glory hole bathtub classroom

———————

gaunt anus in
Cub Scout tub mentioned
at lunch

———————

again in my face
his ass, swelling
and then stopping

———————

teacher spills agonistically

———————

a macho mom, hard
and high, drinking
port—plum eyeshadow

———————

     Max Frisch potluck
stops me cold, a fix of Frisch
meatloaf old hat to cherry
cordial Bachmann before she set
her Rome apartment
on fire—Bachmann and
Lispector self-immolated—
one Jewish, one not

———————

     this is you
outside the burning building
with a burning bush on
the brain—

———————

     after Adrienne
Rich died, I played my class
"A Woman Dead in Her Forties"
recited by the poet

—————

getting off on Brian
Wilson and teaching me
the meaning of late Brian Wilson
artistry at suppertime

—————

dreamt the French professor insisted
on kissing me in the bathroom

—————

whitefishing it up like marriage
and friendliness stored
in a body not remembering its holes

—————

a Saint Sebastian photo
weaving together my first
name's leftover pieces—
when "Way" is missing the
"ne," I become the Italian
part of speech that is
negligibility itself—"ne," shamed

—————

examination dream—
I mentioned gnostic hermeticism
in Paul Klee but
meant hermetic gnosticism
in Georg Trakl

———————

Schoenberg afraid
of the number 13

———————

9 is a gawky number
with pimples and anxiety attacks

———————

water supervised by ramp
crossing over it

———————

Kent jumped off Rip Van
Winkle Bridge into the Hudson
a year after giving me
Poetry and Mysticism

———————

on my back porch
he left the gift and a penciled note—
"this book should blow your mind"

—————

every time I hear the phrase "blow
your mind" I think of his suicide

—————

every night
it pours Purim

—————

the teacher's need
for attention is violent—

—————

why
did they assign me invisible
exercises rather than visible ones?

#31

[tantric opiate for killjoys]

while we're on the subject
of death

_____

emerging nudism bops me
on the head, not far
from dad fingerprints

_____

like the underpants incident,
under his shellac dress
a Marina del Rey
caboose or patio

_____

     plunged
paints without deliberation
on new shiny canvas

_____

do some men have
three balls?

———————

Callas
Gioconda 1960 a surprise—
I thought it was 1952

———————

mother in dream said
her stillborn child was
named Chad

———————

being violated by children
because of inadequate
hors d'oeuvres

———————

junior
high school VP looked like
Nixon or his cronies

———————

my father rumored
to be a soccer star

—————

always saying yes
produces drought

—————

Hedda Nussbaum beaten nose,
daughter a victim of Joel Steinberg

—————

      smashed
flat nose photographed—
my Greenwich Village
where they lived and where
the daughter died

—————

      ate four
walnuts thinking of wide-eyed
Argus and Hedda Nussbaum
eyes seeing daughter's murder

—————

reading about the abuse
I felt soiled—a Greenwich
Village 1980s emotion
connected to rise of ATMs

——————

to consolidate the cloud
death releases, to pierce
the good cloud death unzips

——————

death restricts signals, no
communication over death-wall

——————

I smile gratuitously at
four men a day, or wait
for accidental elbow touch

——————

almost touched butt on
subway—he leaned into
my gloved hand, I
lowered hand and he
kept on leaning

———————

I decided in dream not
to play Sunday's orchestral
concert, I hadn't
practiced trumpet in years

———————

    yet I wanted
to renew my fraudulent
offer

———————

    of foam—
to fill a canvas sequentially
with aporias and dads

———————

    guys with strong
thighs don't accept
feedback—*Lisztomania*
for instance or vibraphone
Lionel Hampton

———————

                    tantric
opiate for killjoys

          ———————

          who is a tart in
this room? all tarts please
stand up and brag

          ———————

          teasing
the bee into epilepsy,
mocking a ladybug and
seeing Lypsinka twice,
Boxed Set plus *Passion of
the Crawford*

          ———————

is anae the plural of
anus, or anii, like
a planet or a dance craze?

          ———————

kid abandoned for nine hours
while father went to work,

father forgot he'd left kid
in locked car, kid died

—————

can't imagine experience
of kid dying all day in a locked,
parked car—remediless

—————

again the cream shadow,
cup custard cookies and dot
cookies, pink speckled succor
in plastic bag, sprinkles fallen
to bag's bottom

—————

every elbow is potential
Messiah

—————

    misname some elbows
Messiah when they're impostors

—————

to spend rest of life listing
failures isn't the secret—
stop listing failures or
stop saying "I failed"

———————

stillbirth dream again—
why was his name
Chad? a violated election,
Gore the stillborn President?
is Chad my stillborn older
brother?

———————

a luxury, to have
a stillborn older President
brother

———————

she observes me
and from bottom
of hierarchy spits upward
in my yolky direction—

———————

Bitsy
the prettiest babysitter, from
a street less frequented,
Happy Valley, near fortress-
hedgerow where beehive mother
and Meissen doll
daughter (a feuding
duo) both taught piano

_____

can't measure
the moods fault-lining Happy Valley

#32

[last call for boy cleft]

wanted
him to solicit my body
instead of my words

————————

triskaidekaphobia
is phobic avoidance of
Triskets

————————

a quitter's
vocation I pursue

————————

make a ceramic
hot plate for Mother's Day
as finger-indented token next
to her sophomore impression-
ability, suicide thoughts
rife in brick quad

————

need polyphonic speech—
ebben as Iago or his
likeness says

————

        the cat
Trakling me into donnée-
focused trance

————

    doomed to answer
fan letters your whole life
because you're a Kennedy
lookalike with long schlong,
a complaining John-John clone

————

Morse code created by inscape
periodicity against straight jock
thigh I violate with
dot-dash trespass

————

Aunt Peggotty
raised Dickens in tablet
or caplet form, 500 mg of
Aunt Peggotty for chronic
lumbago

—————

dead crow
on street and tuna bits
rotten in garbage

—————

the non-boy
cleft is also sometimes
a boy's—last call for
boy cleft

—————

my wife
is John Singer Sargent

—————

like stolen
Klimts and the studly shrink
at Viennese pastry café

for morning transferential
blintz

———————

one judgment per coma,
one coma per jouissance

———————

      he makes new
porn to upload suffering and
re-miserate or trans-
miserate it—resplice
commiserate to tumble it

———————

      tiny hair-like
sliver-grooves inside
rude umber line

———————

I'm not a person, merely
an underneath consciousness
in Nietzsche-reading green
summer Western amphitheater
becoming wise and Übermensch

in minced portions like Swanson
TV dinner Übermensch

———————

create masculinity and then
be smashed snail-like
by its tyrant foxtrot

———————

a couple's cocks—I loved
both or both loved mine,
both seemed especial
connoisseurs of mine

———————

Joan Kennedy played
a Mozart concerto's slow
movement with the Boston
Symphony

———————

call
poetry "abjected" if that
gives you a reason to like
poetry or prevent its suicide

———————

　　　bottomed by a newly
risen top who becomes viewing
booth for freshly hatched
Risorgimento/retrenchment
scenarios—I meant
revanchism? or
another renegade technique?

———————

make sure they kiss me
as my own version of
Nuremberg trial

———————

father writes to say today
would have been his mother's
114th birthday—
also the anniversary
of JFK's assassination—

———————

students saddled with deaths
of their teachers, teachers
dying vocally and in public

―――――――

watched Joan Crawford's
1970 David Frost TV interview
when she mentions Clark
Gable's testicles—
her shoulders my
identification linchpin,
though Edith Head
didn't dress me—

―――――――

  bit in bed
by a spider while I
saw *What's Up, Doc?*
Ryan O'Neal nude and
bronzer-wearing Barbra
in a tub

―――――――

  I discussed
California with Caroline
Kennedy—why didn't
I befriend Caroline, buy a new
wardrobe so I could

present myself to Mrs.
Onassis and hear music
of the spheres as she prepares my
peanut butter and jelly sandwich?

—————

M comes into shower to shake
my nude hand—why didn't
I feel honored?

—————

        and what
happened to loop-haired
daimon-eyed Gentile (tattoo on flank)
complimenting my underwear?

—————

fastidious genital
rhythms unpredictable
like a spumoni ice cream treat
not desired because
the palate has failed
to acquire the spumoni habit

#33

[why all musicians must be lonely]

                Elizabeth
Bishop lived in reach
of Key West graveyard

          _____

          yes V would
let me worship his ass in
stirrups if I could stage
it without revealing my
pallor

          _____

          Mistral the
poet and mistral the wind

          _____

room devoted to mother
arm's terror and value

          _____

half-dead we claim
likeness to full life

—————————

        after Else
Lasker-Schüler was beaten up
she emigrated
to Palestine—buried
on Mount of Olives

—————————

defined and harnessed by
my mouth's ugliness
as seen in college by
Caroline Kennedy's
hypothesized gaze

—————————

Anna Moffo's audition for
Sound of Music (1963?)
heard today for first time
plus *Austerlitz* harpsichord-
accompanied schlocky theme
song, like Morton Feldman
tickled in dark silent room

———————

mother's tuna sandwich in Stickney's
darkness where pie
racks shone, bathroom
corridor's Lucky Strike and Pall
Mall machines

———————

sitting in Miltonic lavatory
for solitude and ease, felix
culpa tearoom—wish I'd
doubled glory-hole usage,
pre-AIDS varieties of
religious jouissance

———————

was
mother's friend Marjie
my art savior? nut-faced
Marjie with mother
after Macy's excursion
—examining purchases
laid out on master bed

———————

living-room bridge
mix with neighbor Gladys

————

      dread of night,
dread of not-night, Kafka
said—weight of drinking and
weight of years of not drinking,
Elizabeth Hardwick said

————

father xeroxes Keats ode
on Xmas as excuse
to exit house and use
pay phone to call mistress

————

Papa didn't watch *Marriage
Italian Style* but I did, and
now I write rather than chat
about normality's intersections
with Simone de Beauvoir

————

please read Arendt's
Totalitarianism alongside Trakl's
poems to discern why
villagers are doxa or
crowd consciousness,
L.A. Frankfurt School re-
make, Schoenberg's "How
One Becomes Lonely"

———————

breakfast
roll in Adorno's mouth as
he asks about global warming

———————

tap dancer Bunny
Briggs died

———————

Mark Strand
died, Monday two weeks ago
saw him walk feebly down
hall, didn't say hello,

never again a chance to
say hello to Mark Strand

———————

mother on a hunger strike

———————

preparing fruit sauce to
accompany cup custards

———————

Eve in dream said
"I have problems,"
bathroom stall not
completely closed in
Hölderlin tower pale
next to law school

———————

               he
is too skinny now, skinniness
removes abjection

———————

    maybe devote
December to sexual hypo-
mania—for what purpose?
to prove death's distance,
paralyze death's wish
to claim me prematurely

———————

Moffo agreed to be
part of documentary—
I'd meet her for the
first time and Henry
would film the encounter—
she died and the meeting
never happened

———————

    before speech
failed her, Eve praised me
in dream—long awkward
silence and then three last
words, "I have problems"—
her complex syntax
eclipsed by sickness

———

      someone's mother
hugged me as
if I were for a moment
a plausible cardboard
fake-son

———

was mother's voice
dodecaphonic?

———

dream—saw (live)
Vivien Leigh test
Streetcar—reading the script
for the first time, opposite
a young Marlon Brando
who resembled Paul Lynde,
cast against type—

———

      I tried to tell
Vivien how sublime
her Blanche was going

to be—impossible
to communicate
her future magnificence

———————

looked at the backs
of her calves—
connected to drowning
in dark green water,
Back Bay, my advocacy
of Hardwick's velvet prose

———————

Mayröcker says a writer
must read for at least
ten hours a day—
photos of May-
röcker, hermit, surrounded
by stacks of books

———————

Guibert's diary
of going blind

———————

Oates's *them*
hardcover (Vanguard
Press) as nirvana
manna eruption
like Lawrence's
The Fox leading
to death scene

———————

                     at market
at first I ignored bok choy,
then decided to buy it

———————

no one else was paying
attention to bok choy

#34

[fronds of a frigged John-Boy]

shirts
unbuttoned, straight
Cain and Abel lump-testing
antediluvian balls

_____

doing imported
laundry for father,
69ing him for "high
five" cultural trauma

_____

fronds of a frigged
John-Boy, contra-
Reich rumination

_____

stringent girl destroys
her lover's toilet paper

_____

          spasm
of retribution *Panis
Angelicus* Franck
sung by Schwarzkopf

_____

          Jesus
washes feet of Apostles
humiliating himself
and raising the ante (auntie?)

_____

     Deborah Kerr
be kind when later
you talk about me

_____

     why
shouldn't gay boy John
be kind when later at the TownHouse
Bar he talks about Deborah Kerr?

_____

connected to Vivien Leigh
dream in Pessoa's house
where I wrote these words

———————

Leigh's chapped
heels seen by me as
Lowell's anti-war
sonnet activism

———————

     don't step
histrionically away
from my predicament
and turn it purple

———————

ephebe's disdain
as I describe
cloacal prose

———————

define for intellectual progeny
the cloacal mother, associated
with sewage

———————

    or else the
cloacal sublime—writing
is a waste product
and therefore disgusts us,
and we choose,
as ethical and lunatic
stance, to form
literature in waste's image—
to write asymptotically
cloacal literature

———————

Robin Williams under-
ground or incinerated
becomes the publicist
of séance and the cloacal
sacrament

———————

I confuse *Undine*
and *Udine*—Undine
is an underwater
mermaid creature,

Udine is an industrial
city in Northern Italy

———————

Schwarzkopf dead and
her name itself
when properly pronounced
is punishment

———————

unlike the
boy in *Molloy* who
receives an enema
from his father

———————

mother in phone message
says "I feel so discouraged"
and I stop listening

———————

handwriting
getting smaller and smaller
in library when I

write my third short
story, "A Peach"—
a son tells his mother
he's gay and then together
they eat a peach

_____

smell of blow job
all over me when I
returned in middle of
night

_____

       his door in
Bauhaus dorm flapping
open

_____

       went
overboard yesterday
on the cloacal
mother—looked up
"cloacal" in my high
school dictionary

———————

       self-video,
hair climbs down in
spider pattern representing
luxury but also a tentacled
failure to be simply itself

———————

the yelp he made
when he came, absence
of self-consciousness

———————

       block kid
Tom says he remembers
my mother always at
kitchen window, stance
signifying education and
watchful contentment

———————

berate my lips because
they are mine, I
wear my lips and so
they are disgusting

_____

like William James
no decent séance-
investigator is disgusted
by butterflies

_____

      HIV was
a patio umbrella
shadow over milk pail
rusty bucket

_____

no amount of
licking his body will
make him Batman

_____

or neutralize the
narrative I'm
bound to repeat

#35

[grandmother taught me futile
or fruitful diphthongs]

does she
bifurcate the noun
to destroy the noun
or to reinforce it?

———————

at urinal
fat man with birthmark
on forehead

———————

guys decorate
guys, guys investigate
decorated guys—
start decorating guys
to destroy or reinforce
Dämmerung

———————

cloacal Pasolini
unslain posing on dog
bench for Ocean Parkway
Sunday blame-fest

———————

Rock Hudson
vigil demands ekphrasis

———————

turning sister into
brother by squeezing brother
and making brother a post-
card and not reinterpreting
the pause in the middle
of brother

———————

Suzanne Juyol my
first Carmen (1951)—
revive her under-
estimated voice

———————

kneeled
in locker room by
tattooed guy putting
on jock strap, cruel face,
no acknowledgment

———————

frozen moment of
mother lifting
nightgown to
admit father

———————

would
she object to the angle?
did he say something
before or after?
just my shoo-fly
father steadying
the light

———————

never seeking to
explore another
man's body, only

wanting incidental
contact, like incidental
music Handel

———————

babysitter found
cigarettes in my
Mattel battery case—
smoked pleasureless,
bathroom window open

———————

mother in bed asked for post
mortem on my junior high dance

———————

father excoriated
"Bumps-muzik"—
his dismissive
term for rock-n-roll—

———————

Walser in sanatorium—
how can asylum
or the ideals of

asylum be woven
into the sentence?

———————

       perceiving
me as mood
cock that will
vibrate her into
better mood

———————

my grandmother
taught me about
futile or fruitful
diphthongs

———————

       fingertips
happy like imperial
Judith Scott
fabric sculpture

———————

poems I tried to
write as finicky descriptions
of *Mandate* men—train
to become abstract
artist by sketching hair

———————

hair doesn't partic-
ipate in sign system,
ipso facto escapes time-line

———————

in Vienna I said
"Hochschule für Musik"
and "conservatoire"—
enigmatically thinking
my shoulders sufficient
exposition whether
hunched or lowered

———————

at whose altar
do I shed my
urge to evolve?

----

in whose shed
do I alter
my urge to revolve?

----

backyard trombone
shed containing Avon lady
Lord Chatters porn
novella, its photo-story
coffers jammed

#36

[crack the fossil carapace of "writer"]

        she thought
us a lovely match
so we became a
lovely match because
she incarnated
corny soundtrack to
Secret Ceremony
not yet seen or made

———————

they necked
and why did I
watch them neck
and why did I freeze
while watching—
into what unsculpted
hell did I descend?

———————

I tried to describe
this abyss but did anyone
listen to my description?

———————

a light blue word-
less painted eggshell

———————

      why does
oil paint look so
desiccated a few
months later? find
ways to retain shine

———————

I was a strange
bonsai who could
play only four pieces—
meager repertoire

———————

Nelson displayed my cock
painting on his shelf

———————

heard Victoria de los Angeles
Manon 1954 Pierre Monteux

———————

         and earlier
Eugene Onegin, Neil
Shicoff's third
season—he specialized
in self-destructive heroes

———————

on the Myers-Briggs
personality chart I'm
an extrovert who
can't push projects
through to completion

———————

*adieu, notre petite
table* and *connais-tu
le pays* my two
new indispensables

———————

tous les deux, together
we'll escape to Paris,
Onegin will slay Lenski,
I'll renounce Onegin
after he changes his
mind and confesses
love for me

———————

Alexander sketched a
dragon quickly and justly—
I can't draw resemblance—

———————

      in dream
John Cage urinated
in bed, bloody
urine at first, then it
landed in his mouth
and he was satisfied

———————

      next to him
in bed, Sturtevant

urinated, her body
(naked) pieced
together from artful
disenchanted emotionally
detached fragments

———————

was she
imitating Cage's
urinating technique?
how did she manage
to urinate a projecting
stream (projective
verse) into her own
mouth?

———————

her shudder-
ing body in cardboard-
colored rickety de-
pressed pieces needing
my respect—

———————

shock that she
was still alive—

———————

shock of Cage urinating
blood, orgasm plasma
autoerotic and expiatory—

———————

Sturtevant mimetic
beside him in bed—
which side of
the bed, mine
or my mother's?

———————

how was the Cage/Sturtevant
bedroom lit? how
could I see the urine
and half-experience it?

———————

I was not present
except as a commiserating
and fearful narrator—

————————

dreamt I bought
Old Spice (reinvented)
cologne or body wash
with a second-rate
singer-actor on
the bottle as sponsor

————————

     also dreamt
Buster Keaton performed
sidewalk pantomime for little kids—
degrading but noble gig

————————

     I protested,
"Buster Keaton is as great
as Chaplin and now he's reduced
to doing sidewalk theater"

————————

     why imagine
I'm Joyce Carol Oates
writing "Accomplished Desires"

or my teenaged mother with legal
pad in Edsel back seat?

———————

    to crack
the fossil carapace
of "writer" and act
freely apart from
carapace—to write
without writing

———————

    I kissed
one guy and then he
left the dim barroom,
so I started kissing
another guy—but when
the original returned
he caught me kissing
the replacement, and
I realized I'd preferred
my first mate—

———————

neither pick-up
had a clear identity—
each was an experiment
in segmented
mortal consciousness
or acting without
fear of consequences
like Jonathan
Edwards and his
spider sphere—

_____

       your orange
coat matches my
sunset

_____

a Jew named Heidi
of Sunnybrook Farm
gobbled up white
bread and vomited it
in pellets to feed
the saxophone
teacher who molested

highway robbers in
the Catskills overlooking
a cold lakeside manu-
facturer of Holocaust
memorabilia for
nutcases

———————

googled
Jason Gould for thirty
minutes yesterday,
looked at pictures of
baby Jason with
mother Barbra—

———————

wish to find at
least one nude
photo of Elliott
Gould before lunchtime,
but googling "Elliott
Gould nude" won't
do any good, I'll
just get fake pictures

———————

      found photo of
Elizabeth Hardwick—remembered
attending Lowell's memorial
service in Emerson
Hall, hearing Bishop read
"The Armadillo"

———————

concentrate on lions,
concentrate on
rabbits and stoats,
concentrate on
a cherub wrapped
in sleet diaper

———————

      write
a line in the bark
of a mountain ash

———————

from its berries
make a jelly

"to protect against
the supernatural"

———————

twenty-three-year-old Moffo
sang Respighi's
La Fiamma in Milan—
1955 recording I discover today—

———————

lower lion into
gladiator pit, eat
lion's armpits, inquire
about son's and
father's simultaneous
puberties and brother's
memorized couplets
heroic or unheroic
for a grammar
school *William Tell*

#37

[for whom the bra tolls]

      opted for no
grilled cheese despite over-
whelming cuteness of grilled
cheese purveyor

_____

      tattooed
fireman without peripheral
vision is leaving

_____

      doesn't turn
around or express the slightest
awareness of other less cute
human beings—

_____

artist named Marnie
Clinton, combo of Tippi
and Hillary, très political

and victim, hands like
Little Richard's

———————

Alessandro
Scarlatti teabagged
Jenny Craig of diet
fame or vice versa,
Jenny Craig teabagged
Alessandro Scarlatti—
visualize it if you will—

———————

tried to find a
church, no church open,
tried to step into the Judson,
homeless guy sleeping in
sacerdotal doorway

———————

my protractor-compass
has a hole in its door

———————

why
do I dream frequently
of Joyce Carol Oates?
what writer do you
frequently dream about?

————————

messy atheist's
self-wounding face scabs

————————

horizontal lines influence
your interpretation
of *Helen and Teacher*

————————

for an hour, steep in your
masculine aura, the most
intoxicating cloud in town

————————

she says "he has a beautiful
mind"—no, he has a
beautiful cock, his mind
is a wasteland of abstractions

––––––––––

how did he end up a
practicing Catholic preoccupied
with incarnation if indeed
he is Jewish? I become
German at these moments,
or at least convinced
of my Germanness

––––––––––

                    don't
wait around for favors
or judge the utterance
while it's happening,
however sere the field
the sentence grows upon

––––––––––

    Sean Connery
(pinch-hitting for Noah)
heard chanteuse
Clementine Abreaction

––––––––––

on her fireplace
Clementine Abreaction
hung a stocking—
it said Christmas Thugs,
which I misread as
Christmas Hugs

———————

Coleridge, beard
marginalia heavy petting

———————

saying "tickle-tickle-teet"
to brother—tickling him
or encouraging him
to tickle my smooth body

———————

for whom the
bra tolls—seeking
the divinatory bra—
running across Hades
or Sahara in search
of *Chinatown* water
(my sister, my daughter)

————

the Israeli
said goodbye to M
but not to me

————

explore through
flattery his stomach and
biceps, say "your body has
improved" and find the secret
of its improvement, let
fingers go beneath shirt
in subtle cyberwarfare

————

torture
today revealed by CIA,
salary increase
for waterboarding

————

knees
apart because father died
when son was seven

―――――

how did block
kid Dougie's dad
die? heart attack? suicide?

―――――

Wally killed
himself—maybe more than
one suicide on our street—
why did I think ours was
the only unhappy family?

―――――

Jane Freilicher
died, revolutionary landscapes

―――――

she might have understood
my island predilection—
the grimy circuit
language makes
in body, round
trip from mouth to mouth—

———————

the foiled voice's
foul agon
a gone foal

#38

[camp marmalade on toast points]

I ate red hots and
couldn't find water
to soothe burnt mouth

———————

parents were "running the
soft water" which meant no
tap water

———————

early morning
I wasn't allowed to
open the refrigerator

———————

didn't even
consider waking my parents or
invading the forbidden fridge
to find milk, Hi-C,
Hawaiian Punch, ginger ale

———————

from Minute Maid frozen
concentrate, plop,
out comes orange juice
barrel-turd (like jellied
cranberry sauce) into pitcher

———————

Flintstones
or Chocks pastel chalky
kid vitamins versus
mother's benny-red
One A Day

———————

did father take a
vitamin pill? no, I don't
remember father ever
eating breakfast

———————

father wants to add vanilla
to French toast batter
and mother forbids him

——————

                her tiny
Concentrate flakes dissolving
in blue skim milk

——————

                skim
milk is terrifying, a watery
ideology—its Troy
Donahue blueness
the base or the superstructure?

——————

                        milk's relation
to its nerdy skimming
is tautological

——————

black conveyer belt
moving at grocery
store when I put condolence
card on its rubber and Bea
the checkout woman consoles
father because I've bought

a condolence card for mother,
hospitalized to give
birth to baby brother—

————————

on Bea's conveyor belt
cantaloupe, V8 juice, chops, fish
sticks, Rice-A-Roni,
Hamburger Helper, orange
sherbet (Safeway brand)
and three-layer ice cream
carton—also
spumoni, incomprehensible—

————————

spumoni at Paesano's
pizza parlor with ground
beef extra cheese pizza

————————

      earlier was Me-n-Ed's
thin pizza, pale cheese,
death disclosed in dark
restaurant, and I didn't realize
Me-n-Ed's meant "me *and* Ed"

————————

      I thought "Me-n-
Ed's" was a word like
mayonnaise or meager
or Massachusetts or
milquetoast or meander—

————————

      Dougie's father's
death notice in newspaper
no relation to pizza-wheel's mandala

————————

Rondine big breast blow
job in baby brother's bedroom
while mother screams

————————

Delta of Venus Nin
Rhys master-bedroom mother
shelf *No More Masks!* she
says Rukeyser knowledgeably

————————

Renata Tebaldi's
early todayness or yesterday-
ness thanks you for clinical
ovation

———————

woman's coat
orange (lox) on street was
contribution to city's
optimism quota

———————

hunger for virtues
Guyotat's beat-sheet intermittently
represents

———————

want Pseudo-Dionysius
the Areopagite to leave
bathroom and excite me
with his upper arms
that earlier ignored me

———————

commas signify diseased
relationship to literature

————————

       Victoria
de los Angeles agrees—

————————

watching word-ponds
form in brain integument

————————

       rooming
inside psychosis because that's
where I choose to live

————————

December 17, father
writes to say "today
is my father's birthday (1905) and
Simón Bolívar's death day (1830)"

————————

Eden was always morning, in
Eden there was no night

———

coin
in Halloween UNICEF cup

———

mother
valued broad chests, my
large lexical shoulders,
adjective nipples

———

mother court-martialed me,
showed a videotape
of court-martialing

———

mention
Valéry without earning
the right to mention Valéry

———

mouth tastes
strange, shop for a new
mouth

————

        spread
camp marmalade on
toast points

————

        purgatory disguised
as JFK fitness-test push-ups

————

        faraway
objects are verbal—
nearby objects
are visual

————

my fourth-grade teacher
was Mrs. Nigh

————

        we never
verified the existence
of Mr. Nigh

#39

[an ample beard I never push to fruition]

lonely dog
barks upstairs, one bark
every twenty seconds

———————

sometimes
the barks come in clusters
of two—bark bark,
bark bark

———————

prolific
minimalist dog

———————

is the first bark
an inhale and the second
bark an exhale?

———————

                    I was
doubtless a demanding
baby—ugly mouth,
vituperative verbal
ass, alternately cramped
and multi-volumed

        _____

                the lid
clamps down
on the Dutch oven—
a spoon seeks its natural
mate, the bowl

        _____

an ample beard I
never push to fruition

        _____

throat constricted,
I bought a gas mask
today, in case I
want to sand

        _____

drapes close with a
totalitarian thwack

———————

to love Kandinsky
but never discover
how to confirm the filiation

———————

plaints constitute themselves
as plaints because they
are twinned

———————

"otiose" is my grandfather's
gift—words piled up to
impress Brooklyn sire

———————

I wait for
regard from a bi source

———————

Albert York
borrowed from Manet

three peach
brush strokes

—————

Virna Lisi died today, co-star
with Jack Lemmon

—————

    brother
left rosettes of Kleenex strewn
across his adolescent bedroom
floor—snowfall
I unkindly raged against

—————

    great-aunt blew
nose like Tannhäuser
squawk

—————

    a novel demands
concentration on
consecutiveness—poetry
entails fussy
babysitting of minutiae

----

      mother
gazed at me through
magnifying glass of grandfather

----

      burned by solar
patriarchal magnification

----

      watching Jack
LaLanne with mother—did
we copy his calisthenics?

----

on same black-and-white TV
JFK funeral unspooling

TV on red brick fireplace with
andirons and *Sunset* magazine
lamp's three askew torchères
like lit nebulae or a hair-drying

orgy—four gilt plastic statuettes
commemorating our births,
delivery times engraved

———————

I have a uterine
Imaginaire and a wish
to summarize a baby gurgling

———————

dream
sex with a hooker bodybuilder—
or are we making an LP,
our faces on the disc's
central label?

———————

Europe's Frank Sinatra
died, Udo Jürgens, deaf
in left ear after Nazi
Jungvolk leader struck him—
Jean Arp was his uncle

———————

                    father
says mother was
psychotic and unreachable
after stillbirth

            ———————

to stretch threshold
experiences, break
a word apart through pun
and somnolence—

            ———————

            Bach's B
minor Mass my mother sang in,
Radcliffe Choral Society, Boston
Symphony Orchestra, March 27,
1949, Serge Koussevitzky

            ———————

brought her a pizza and
a mandarin orange

            ———————

she wants to choose a
middle name for herself

———

the two choices are Faith
and Edna—Faith because
that might have been her middle name
if her parents had bothered
to give her a middle name—
and Edna because of Edna
St. Vincent Millay

———

St. Vincent's Hospital,
now defunct,
where I healed
from my electrocution

———

almond candy in white
lace, a nuptial favor
brought home to me by
mother, who derided
cold cuts at neighbor-girl's
wedding feast—

———

heard this afternoon
Victoria de los Angeles
1958 singing Desdemona,
Fausto Cleva conducting,
March 1958, six months
before my birth

————————

also 1970
Tebaldi/Tucker *Bohème*,
again Fausto Cleva,
last time Tebaldi and
Tucker sang a Met
broadcast together—
I was twelve years old

————————

too tired to give the context
that might make the
detail matter, and now its
undescribed context falls
murdered and neglected
into the pit

————————

tonight mother said
she wants a foster child,
but then later after I
brought a pizza she said
she didn't want a foster child

———————

because I
had the wherewithal to
bring her a pizza, she'd
forego the pleasure and ease
of a foster child, whose
purpose might have been
to deliver pizzas

#40

[persimmon solar couture]

       working with Evelyn Waugh
and Yves Montand on a
Zoetrope underground remake
of *Help!* and *Torch
Song Trilogy* in Poland

—————

       posing as a
model in persimmon solar
couture

—————

Moffo in dream released
a four-record Fauré *mélodies* set—

—————

she approved or disapproved
of my career, and rose
to consciousness as a round-
faced foible, an *I can't*—

———————

fantasy of reconnecting
with sophomore boyfriend,
yarmulke on kouros-
coiled hair in Facebook wedding photo

———————

     wonder if I was
his only boyfriend and if he
has good memories of my legs

———————

noticing my legs when
we jogged

———————

     Nijinsky's cock
or midsection surgically
cleft by lightning
or governmental fiat

———————

       cascading
ferns over glass-fountain

walls, a Miró vision, but
who will side with Miró
before he becomes Miró?
who will endorse and ratify
his visions before they
become hotel decor?

———————

before
they were decor, they
were infamy and shame,
moons and vectors
not floral and not
metaphoric

———————

gumming a piece of
shrimp, she wants more shrimp
but still has three
shrimps on plate

———————

we left one orange in
her room, three bananas
beside the TV

———

       father demanded
mother give back
engagement ring during
divorce trial

———

       encourage her to
produce true and odd phrases
and help her compile
sentences and strategize
their collusion

———

       dine
at bygone pancake restaurant
conjoined with gas station

———

       only briefly did
that auto-pancake constellation
exist, and then it died

———

Tinker's Damn, gay
bar on Saratoga Avenue—
wanting blow job
at fourteen, an early start

————

nonexistent biceps
need Bullworker supplement
in eighth-grade summer—
never ordering Bull-
worker and not knowing
how to order it

————

mother says she and sister
have the same build

————

green
dress with noodle-soup stain

————

floppy cornhole of
antique dealer—we watch

video or Super 8 porn
in Walnut Creek bed—
his aperture easy, uncrinkled

————————

sometimes a small
moment of interaction
seems divinely sticky
and intentional—

————————

           clean-
shaven man reading
financial pages and shaking
his leg

————————

        wanting
to intrude a curious
investigative hand on other
men's bodies in public—
to scrutinize their lumps,
folds, punishable irregularities

————————

sometimes my smile is
crooked—work on
making it symmetrical

———————

right eye
perpetually leaking

———————

in dreams
fathers wear boxers with
secret password—
open sesame

———————

boxers
open to admit poetic
complexity like pears or
rude violets

———————

nudes
are never rude
in violet's
inviolate zone

———

I did an imper-
sonation of a Barbra im-
personation

———

dreamt masseur said
wise embittered things about
faculty politics

———

      beaten up in junior
high gym class—did that
give my father Nazi
flashbacks?

———

      mother saying let
your vanquished rival
sit with you at lunch,
he doesn't have anyone
else to sit with

———

a mere, Amir,
a *mère* terror,
amère for
bitterness, *amertume*,
a bitter tomb

#41

[hype for Ben's frum lump]

never too Atget, never too
blurred or precise, never too
solicitous of lost Parisian
avenues and haberdasheries,
never too delineated
and elegiac, never too hearsay-
oriented and Offenbach

———————

little boy eats fruit bowl
and scrambled eggs with his fingers

———————

    my teacher's
name she said was Mrs.
Marcus, "a tragic figure with
circles under her eyes"

———————

    pancake
and waffle chopped up

————

she said
father joined the Vedanta society
sophomore year—switched
from physics to philosophy—
wrote dissertation on
Bertrand Russell and mysticism—

————

and then I smile at a man
for scientific experiment's sake—
I like to watch men
make the transition from
indifference to friendliness

————

we smelled wild fennel
near the tower, saw irises or
violets or pansies or heliotrope,
yes heliotrope, in the park
beside the toilet a few
yards north of the ruined
church we made up our
minds to drive south to
ward off the Spanish flu

———

on Filbert Street
wore tight punk
shirt, low-cut, in-
timated that I'd spend
the night with him—
without words he refused

———

in a story I described
his skin's guest-soap smell

———

   stopped
at the baths on my way
back home, an hour,
attempting recompense—
burning devil mural
on entrance wall

———

   rent a locker
not a cubicle, wander down
halls past opened doors,
surrender to generic invitation

———

blue jellies made
my heels bleed

———

take glazing seriously
as a systematic pursuit

———

dreamt PJ told me to
submit a book to *SMI*
(sadomasochism *c'est moi?*)

———

remembering
mother discussing D&C
with father in station
wagon—I couldn't
define a D&C—

———

itched ear repeatedly
with a fingertip stained
Rose Madder, transparent,

as opposed to Fanchon
Red, partially opaque—

———————

                God
exists by tearing himself
in half says Simone
Weil

———————

        stultification
versus emancipation says
Rancière, and a body
agrees to stultify itself

———————

I will engage in one
hour of emancipation today
and one hour of stultification
tomorrow

———————

a yarmulke and a bobby
pin holding it nervously
in place on West 23rd

———

  mother calls
herself a cheap date, Chinese
food 25 cents in 1952

———

  married at Hotel
St. George, Brooklyn Heights,
1952, engagement announced
in *Daily Eagle*, newspaper
my grandfather wrote for

———

  Wittgenstein
destroyed my career,
so said father while eating
smoked salmon crêpe
at Venezuelan restaurant

———

dreamt of Julie Andrews
photo, a revealing bra

———

Ben's crotch
lump sticks out—he sang
"Edelweiss"

————————

never too much
hype for Ben's lump

————————

nude scenes in *Sound
of Music* with an adult
lump or a kid lump or a
petition to undo or interpret
Ben's philosophic
midnight lump

————————

Richard Tauber died of
cancer after singing Don
Ottavio in 1947, Vienna
State Opera, a guest star—
left Germany in 1933

————————

still curious about Ben's
lump and would love him
to acknowledge that I'm
looking inquisitively at it

————————

she entered death for
a full hour to learn
its architecture

————————

how
do I know whether death
will release me after
the experimental hour?

————————

a snack death,
not a full meal

————————

Ajaccio
violets of a lump
observer

_____

three minutes of Craigslist
M4M, frum for frum

_____

        Luise Rainer
died, 104 years old,
Switzerland—two
Academy Awards con-
secutively for *The Great
Ziegfeld* and *The Good Earth*

_____

        but if I'm
not frum can I pose as
frum and answer the frum
for frum ad?

#42

[as if seen through a junk bottle]

the injunction to avoid
nudes is a punishing downer

———————

I'm hungry and might
not be able to make
it through this notebook

———————

an event for which
I am vulgarly overdressed

———————

before Dickinson died
she wrote "Called back"

———————

Magda Olivero is the
new high point of the 20th
century though during

the 20th century I was
under-aware of her splendor

———————

giving direction to a leaf,
Thoreau noticed a "tchip tchip"
sound and a specific pink
or loud-voiced man

———————

Thoreau:
"I was thinking, accidentally,
of my own unsatisfactory life"

———————

"There is no life
perceptible on this broad meadow
except what I have named"

———————

Dickinson was
wrong about the rainbow

———————

Jackie Onassis had post-traumatic
stress disorder and I travel
down that tunnel for hours

_____

Magda Olivero inserted
messa di voce everywhere

_____

like Margaret Cho's mother
discovering "Ass Master"
on the first page

_____

the beckoning composition
in blue (Kandinsky?)
was first catalyst—

_____

blue I
wrote about on Kirkland Street
steps

_____

was autumn-torn
sunlight, not blue, the catalyst?

————————

Thoreau:
"as if seen through /
a junk bottle"

————————

sifting = halo

————————

like my
fictional characters I
am dead and in search of
vulcanian vampiric
consolation—like Nosferatu
mixed with Julia Child

————————

why didn't I say
please drop your towel?

————————

        father in boxers
with egregiously
muscular calves—

        _____

        did she lie
down to show me
three holes or am I
remembering "bare ruin'd"
beige carpet,
landing strip for airplane
memory of vaginal
structure explained?

        _____

        like sugary
sprinkles on coffee cake
when I'm allowed
intimate lunch (tuna melt?)
at Blum's while brother
duets with violinist—charity
concert at old-age home

        _____

                    electric
toothbrush (mother's)
for jerk-off—did I wash
the toothbrush afterward?

          ―――――

her bedroom door
white and vacuum-sealed,
a soundproof folding screen—

          ―――――

          bed my
parents slept in,
rattan basket weave
magazine and pajama
compartment behind
heads, *Time Newsweek*
Ramparts

          ―――――

father on left,
mother on right—
mornings while
father made breakfast

mother moved
to the left and
slept with mouth open,
blood crust around lip rims

———————

    do I remember the
first day of kindergarten,
yes, I remember the first
day of kindergarten, am
I ashamed to remember
the first day of kindergarten,
yes, I am ashamed to
remember the first day of
kindergarten, what happened
the first day of kindergarten,
nothing happened the first
day of kindergarten

———————

passive eyes sunk
in sockets, lintel of bone

———————

first years of writing
in childhood bedroom
after reading Nin's *House*
of Incest and listening to
Adrienne Rich poetry-
reading LP, the record
mother later broke in
half at quarrel's climax

———————

       sundered pieces
I pitied—

———————

       call this book
Shifting Sands at
Windhover or *Glancing*
Toward Mother's Entrails
or *Why a Father Perplexes*
the United States or
Timeshares in an Alaskan
Hereafter or *Taboos*
for Breakfast or
Tantamount to Ecstasy
or *Starlings as Tomboys*—

----

no, just *A Star Hit
My Noggin* or
In Search of Lost Orifices
or *Buster Keaton's
Embouchure* or
Pillage and Crêpe
or *Testing Mr. Fayrechild*
or *If Eden Changed
Its Mind*—no,
just *Orgasms by the
Dozen* or *Pennywhistle Orgasms*

----

the clock in the dining
room had no love for us—
the clock befriended the thermostat

----

beside their bed
was there always a door, or
did it materialize *in medias res*?

----

a communist
door, announcing strangeness

_____

don't romanticize their door,
it had no erotic charge

_____

in the house
flanking ours, Betty
wept—her husband died
so she keened at night

_____

she said "Betty has go to
the bathroom" when we took
her out to dinner as charity—
excuse Betty, she needs
to go to the bathroom
because her husband died
and this nerdy obnoxious
Jewish family is taking her
out to dinner to celebrate
or salve her solitude

_____

an accordion player
became her lover—at night
I overheard his polkas—
through my bedroom
window I spied the couple
frolicking in Betty's bathroom

———————

learn German
so I can live in a German
mouth—the only way to
function happily is within
German vowels as forgiveness
plaints, preserved in a hornbook

———————

the newcomer took off
his underwear and apologized,
said "I'm bulking up"—I
should have immediately
said "no you have the body of
a god"—if I say right away
"you have the body of a
god" I'll get farther

———————

doch means not
dock not port
not doctor

———————

dreamt
the poet gave an end-of-life
lecture, half-cross-dressed,
dick showing through negligee

———————

the man
in a wheelchair said
Gravity and Grace is a
great title—I said
I didn't know whether
she chose that title or
whether it was posthumously
chosen—I pronounced Weil
the French way, VAY

———————

I should have
said VEIL, to veil one's
wares, and once a week
attend a collective
nude gathering

—————

how can I tell if my
painting is finished?
call it *Break of Day*
after Colette and
her mother and the
six yellow suns
shining without self-
consciousness at the rectangle's
optically disorienting
bottom—

—————

in my hand
a round small
not attractive lemon

—————

earlier
I ignored the lemon,
didn't feel attached to it

———————

like when the guest wiggled his ass
and I was supposed to find
the spectacle rivetingly sexy but felt
instead "contact shame"

———————

lemon not entire,
lemon with a crease
I caused, proof
of my negligence—

———————

please explain
what you mean
by negligence

———————

I will explain
later, after I finish

singing a lament
for the lemon

——————

"manufactory" my
great-aunt Alice called
her father's candy-
making enterprise in
19th-century Berlin—

——————

maybe not a factory, maybe
just a shop, or one
room with till and stove
for ensuring that his goodies-
in-process attained
the boiling point—

——————

    1970s, on her table
a plate of bologna and Port
Salut, and a fruit bowl

——————

              her favored
books the autobiographies
of Golda Meir and
Arthur Rubinstein

———————

I can't find the
notebook where I
originally wrote
the phrase "sifting = halo"

———————

maybe it was a quote
from Benjamin's hashish
protocol or Thoreau's
1839 journal—

———————

or maybe the phrase
"sifting = halo" is my own

———————

by sifting do we
discover halo?

———————

does halo
withdraw its presence
after it has taught
us how to sift?

———————

what good is our knowledge
of how to sift, if
we can no longer
find the halo
whose luminous enigma
drove us to divide
useful from useless droplets?

———————

we learn to
incarnate halo
by sifting

———————

even if the cloud
we sift turns out
not to be a halo

———

our obligation
is to elevate
the atmosphere
into a halo through
the fastidiousness
or recklessness of
our sifting—

———

we nominate
the mere cloud
a halo though it
never presented
halo credentials

———

and thus we justify
our habitual reliance
on the never-to-be-
defined activity
of sifting

———

as if by sifting
we could impose
a rift in raw
experience, and
separate its troubled
from its untroubled face—

————————

no captor, no
creator exists
to measure the ardor
or listlessness of my
halo decipherment

————————

did the halo
ask to be disturbed
by the nervous
actions of a sifter?

————————

does the halo
exist only as echo
of a sifter's
insatiate murmurings?

———————

        now, please,
reconceive the nature
of the sieve *I am*—

———————

and through its neutral net

———————

behold the fine
and coarse particles
bewildered fall

Acknowledgments

The author thanks the editors of the following publications (print and online), in which portions of this book, sometimes in different versions, appeared:

Academy of American Poets (Poem-a-Day): "#21 [the old soiled carpet of the wish to be Anaïs]"

Adult Contemporary: "#14 [tight ultramarine fealty to wimp identity]"

Dia: Readings in Contemporary Poetry: "#12 [the dematerializing marzipan]"

FOLDER: "#11 [slaughter ball]," "16 [a pear blue green slivered near brown]"

FourTwoNine: "#3 [nocturne for a cut-up dad]"

Hotel: "#2 [elegant toplessness stoned in stairwell]"

Numéro Cinq: "#15 [imprisoned within Busby Berkeley or the ethereal phlox]," "#20 [thick book on mother-shelf pinnacled me o'er Tums]"

*

"#1 [I despise always trying to be an intellectual]" was published as a chapbook by The King Library Press

(University of Kentucky Libraries) in 2015, with the assistance of Stuart Horodner, Paul Holbrook, and David Elbon.

*

Special thanks to Stephen Motika, to Lindsey Boldt, to Jeff Clark, to Filipa Calado, to Emma Jacobs, and to everyone who encouraged the continuing trance.

Wayne Koestenbaum has published nineteen books of poetry, nonfiction, and fiction, including *Notes on Glaze, The Pink Trance Notebooks, My 1980s & Other Essays, Hotel Theory, Best-Selling Jewish Porn Films, Andy Warhol, Humiliation, Jackie Under My Skin*, and *The Queen's Throat* (a National Book Critics Circle Award finalist). He has had solo exhibitions of his paintings at White Columns (New York), 356 Mission (L.A.), and the University of Kentucky Art Museum. His first piano/vocal record, *Lounge Act*, was issued in 2017 by Ugly Duckling Presse Records. He is a Distinguished Professor of English, French, and Comparative Literature at the CUNY Graduate Center in New York City.

Nightboat Books

Nightboat Books, a nonprofit organization, seeks to develop audiences for writers whose work resists convention and transcends boundaries. We publish books rich with poignancy, intelligence, and risk. Please visit our website, www.nightboat.org, to learn about our titles and how you can support our future publications.

The following individuals have supported the publication of this book. We thank them for their generosity and commitment to the mission of Nightboat Books:

Elizabeth Motika
Benjamin Taylor

In addition, this book has been made possible, in part, by grants from the National Endowment for the Arts and the New York State Council on the Arts Literature Program.